COACH
YOURSELF
TO
WIN

*Dedicated to my Mum, whose unwavering support
has been with me since my very first book.*

COACH
YOURSELF
TO
WIN

Jon Emmett

FERNHURST
BOOKS

A catalogue record for this book is available from the British Library
ISBN 978-1-909911-21-5

Front cover image: *Lijia Xu winning Gold in the Laser Radial Class at the London 2012 Olympic Games* © Clive Mason / Getty Images
Back cover image by Chen Jun
All photographs by Jon Emmett, except:
p5 & 69 by Chen Jun; p14 & 31 by Tim Davison / Dave Giles

Designed by Rachel Atkins
Illustrated by Karl Brandt
Printed in China through World Print

JON EMMETT

GOLD MEDAL WINNING COACH & SAILOR

Jon Emmett is a professional sailing coach who coached Lijia Xu to win Gold in the Laser Radial class at the London 2012 Olympic Games. He is also the Training Officer for the UK Laser Class Association.

As well as coaching, Jon is a very successful and regular competitor, with successes including:

Byte C II Class
* World Champion
* European Champion

Laser Radial Class
* Masters World Champion (twice, including the year of writing)
* Masters European Champion (twice)
* Europa Cup Series Winner (twice)
* UK National Champion (6 times)
* UK National Ranking Series Winner (over 10 times)
* UK Inland National Champion (over 10 times)

Coach Yourself to Win is a re-written, more focused version of Jon's popular title *Be Your Own Sailing Coach* (available as an eBook), and builds on his vast experience as a gold medal winning coach. Jon is also author of Fernhurst Books' *Be Your Own Tactics Coach*.

www.jonemmettsailing.co.uk

Also by the author:

Be Your Own Tactics Coach

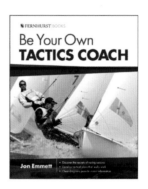

A comprehensive programme to make you a tactical genius.

CONTENTS

FOREWORD

I first knew Jon Emmett from his well-renowned book, *Be Your Own Sailing Coach*. This book has helped thousands and thousands of wonderful sailors to reach their dreams by improving themselves to be all-round sailors by following his detailed instructions. That included me – a Chinese sailor who was extremely thirsty to acquire comprehensive knowledge about sailing. That book imparted me with all the knowledge I needed to know as a professional sailor, but at the same time I was not satisfied and I wanted to further improve myself and become an Olympic Champion.

I was so lucky to have Jon as my coach towards the 2012 Olympic campaign. I have never got on so well with a coach like him before. He not only has a nice personality and character to work with, but he is also super competent in numerous roles, far beyond a sailing coach: such as acting as a psychologist to help sailors prepare mentally for competitions, as a meteorologist to analyse the weather conditions, as a nutritionist to plan a good diet for athletes, as both a personal trainer and partner when doing gym exercises to improve sailors' fitness, as a physio to give advice for sports treatment and injury prevention tips, and so on. Overall he is a very efficient person and, apart from being a fantastic sailing coach, can help many members of the team to build good relationships and a great team spirit.

Jon knows exactly how sailors feel and what sailors want for the simple reason that he is still an active sailor by training and participating in various regattas every year. That's why he understands the sailors more than many other coaches. He also really listens to them – the quality of communication between him and the sailors helps to secure effective training and progression all the time.

It was Jon who helped me to win the Olympic Gold in the London Games, and it is without doubt that this book will be a blessing for all sailors who read it. An excellent coach, he will give every reader the best value in sailing knowledge by sharing his experience and suggestions.

I hope that all of you who love sailing can achieve higher levels with the help of this book, and welcome whatever challenge the future may bring. Enjoy!

Lily (Lijia Xu)
Laser Radial Gold Medallist, London 2012

CHAPTER 1

Targets & Goal Setting

This book is for all those busy people who still want to be successful, and need to optimise every hour of every training session without a coach!

Not many people complain about having too much time on their hands. Sailing, like any sport, rewards hours of quality training. We want to make sure that any time we invest in our sailing is used as usefully as possible. One of the reasons why it is so hard to improve your racing is that sailing is such a time-intensive sport. It could take you many hours to arrive at the sailing venue, rig up the boat and get out on the water, whilst a runner or cyclist may be able to commence a great training session the moment they close their front door.

The aim of this book is to help everyone improve their skills in the shortest possible time, and this requires focus. When you go on a journey, to reach your destination you need to look at the map and plan the best route, not blindly head off in any direction. This means that you need to (assess yourself to) know where you are, and also know where you need to get to (your goals).

Coaching is a huge part of professional training – having someone to help with the analysis and give a second opinion – but for many sailors access to a professional coach is something that happens rarely or not at all and this is where this book can help.

After more than twenty years of coaching it made sense to put all of the most effective training exercises and key ideas into a book which will undoubtedly help you get towards the front of the fleet whether your goal is Club, National, International or even Olympic level. The same proven techniques will help you wherever you are in your sailing career.

Why are Goals so Important?

Well firstly, if you don't have a clear target, how do you know when you have achieved something? Humans by nature like a sense of achievement: think of all the opportunities to win badges, certificates and awards when we are young (or indeed as we get older the targets, such as getting a degree, become bigger and better).

They provide motivation: if something is too easy ("my aim for today is to clean my teeth") then there is very little feeling of accomplishment, or if something is too hard (or perhaps impossible, like running your first marathon in under two hours) it will lead to disappointment, and repeated failure can be hard to bear. The idea is to set yourself a rewarding challenge, something you can achieve if you really put your mind to it.

The purpose of this book is to break your overall sailing goal down into small and manageable mini-goals. After all it is impossible for a human to eat an elephant in one go but if divided into small enough pieces and given enough time, then, anything is possible.

Things which are measured are more likely to be achieved, as at the end you have proof that you achieved them (or not). This is why taking detailed records of the weights you lift is so important – so you can see where you came from, what you have achieved and what you need to do next. Try to learn skills in the easiest possible way, using a method than helps you remember what you learnt. For example, in my book *Be Your Own Tactics Coach*

I use character names (like Terry Tacker who tacks on every shift) as lots of research has shown that this is a very good way of remembering things.

Visual aids are also an excellent way of seeing information at a glance: not only is it much clearer than just rows and columns of numbers, but it is more rewarding to look at!

The key to improving your overall sailing ability is to work on your weaknesses. A good way to understand where your weaknesses lie is to compare your abilities in a number of areas in a single visual form.

The issue is: we tend to enjoy what we are good at and are therefore more inclined to practise it (and get even better at it) and dislike what we are not good at (and therefore not practise it and not improve at it). To improve our overall ability effectively, our training routines should be the other way round – focusing on our weaker areas.

However there may be some events where you would choose to specialise, for example preparing for a championship which will be held only in strong winds due to the expected sailing conditions. This may mean that you could, for that season, neglect your light wind training, if only the result in this one regatta was important to you.

Dartboards

Filling out a dartboard is very simple. You start from the middle and colour one or more sections depending upon how comfortable you feel with that skill: 1 = very low skill (no colour would be no skill at all!) and 10 would be perfect. It is not really how you choose to rate yourself (which often shows more your confidence rather than your competence) but the *differences* in how you rate yourself in the individual areas.

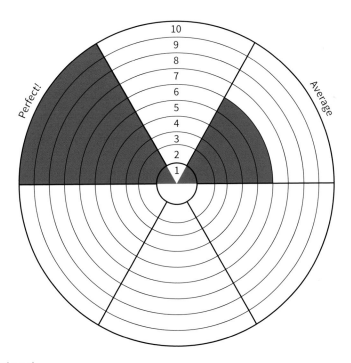

How to fill out a dartboard

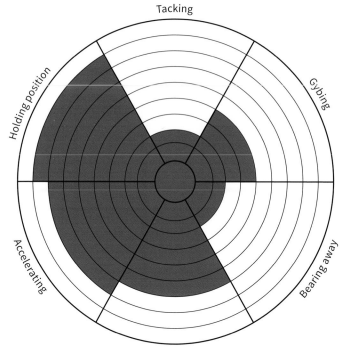

An example of a boat handling dartboard

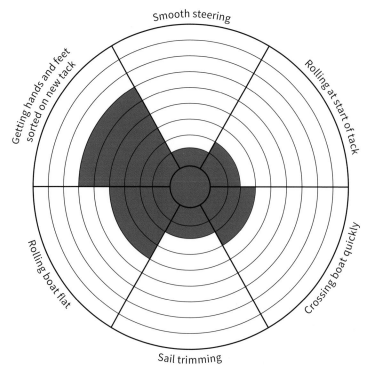

An example of a tacking dartboard

An example of a tacking exercises dartboard

You can, of course, make as many or as few dartboards as you like, but the more specific and the more detailed they are the better. So consider Chapter 2: Boat Handling: we could create a dartboard showing six key areas for all the boats we are racing (opposite, top). Perhaps having recently changed to a trapeze boat we are struggling to tack, gybe and bear away, but we are already confident to hold position, accelerate and head up.

Now we have identified some of the areas we want to work on (and boat handling is often a very good example of an issue we could expect when changing to a new class) we can go into more detail. So then we look at tacking (opposite, bottom), as it (along with bearing away), we decided, is the weakest area and therefore where we can get some rapid improvement. This dartboard clearly shows the specific areas we need to work on.

Now we can finally choose some actions to help us. This is so much more effective than just going sailing and 'practising boat handling'. The final dartboard (above) shows some exercises that we can do to help our steering, body movement and sheeting. Those exercises which require us to do lots of tacks, such as riverboat, can be more useful than tacking on the whistle as they require more thought, whilst tacking in a race can hide your weakness as, even in a short race, boatspeed can help compensate for your poor tacks.

Most useful is when you do very detailed exercises like tying your tiller (so that you cannot steer using the rudder), fixed sheet tacking (so that you cannot steer using the sheet) or bum in the boat (not in this dartboard, but where you cannot move your body) which soon identify where the biggest issues lie and therefore where your time should be spent. Time management is a very important skill in modern life and you should keep careful records of your training to make sure it is paying off.

So good luck, train hard and enjoy the rest of the book.

CHAPTER 2

Boat Handling

The phrase 'boat handling' refers to any skills that are not directly related to straight line speed. These can often be practised on land where the boat is securely tied to the trolley and you can analyse very carefully what is best to do with your hands and feet with no risk of a capsize.

The important thing is to be able to perform near perfect boat handling manoeuvres under pressure as this gives you lots of tactical options. For example, if you know that you can tack under someone without being rolled, or if you can gybe quickly making it hard for someone to cover you (or easier for you to cover them). You do so many tacks and gybes over the course of a race: if you can make each one just ⅓ boat length better, accumulatively that is a huge distance by the end of the race, and many fewer points at the end of a series.

It is also worth noting that slow speed boat handling skills, like those required pre-start, are very important too. It is not all about achieving rapid acceleration: being able to slow down, hold position and turn without going over a start line are all very important.

Practice

Practice makes perfect so, if you think of all the boat handling that you do during the course of a race, it is obvious that boat handling drills are an essential part of any campaign. When sailing high performance boats for the first time, just being able to get around the race course in the upper wind range can be a real achievement (and it is perhaps worth making sure that your first couple of sails are done in light to medium breezes!).

It is advisable to get your boat handling to a reasonable level before you hitch your boat up to go to your first open meeting as you cannot race effectively if your boat handling is not up to scratch (your strategy and tactics will be compromised if you cannot tack / gybe or get around the marks efficiently).

That old cliché: 'time on the water' is definitely true when it comes to perfecting boat handling, but remember that the more specific and demanding you make the exercises, the greater the potential improvement. By doing a good range of exercises (rather than simply going out and tacking and gybing) it is possible to keep motivation high, and old skills can soon be remembered again with intensive practice. In fact practising boat handling can be an excellent way of developing specific fitness (like doing fast spinnaker hoists and drops).

Don't Apply the Brake

Using the rudder to correct the steering of a boat (forcing it to sail in a straight line when it wants to luff up or bear away) makes the rudder act as a brake. Therefore any boat will probably be sailing at its fastest when using minimum corrective steerage.

Even in classes like the Laser, where you do lots of downwind turns, you still want to do this with minimal rudder movement (instead using the crew weight and sheeting to get the boat to turn).

Remember that when you are sailing in a straight line the boat needs to be kept flat. You can prove this to yourself by (briefly) letting go of the tiller and seeing if the boat carries on in a straight line.

When the boat is turning corners you will, of course, need some rudder movement, but as much as possible you want the rudder to follow the boat's turn (which is caused by crew weight and sheeting) rather than aggressive pushing or pulling of the tiller! Often the more body movement the better, as this is your opportunity to put some energy into the boat. You need to be controlled but aggressive – so big movements, but remember to keep them smooth.

Tacks & Gybes

The first thing we need to do is define what a good **tack** is (much like before the days of sat navs we used to have to look at a road map to decide the best route to take before setting off). A good tack is simply one where you continue to make maximum progress upwind. For example, if you try to tack too quickly, then you are likely to lose speed in the tack.

There will be times when you simply need to tack as quickly as possible, perhaps because you overstood a layline, or you needed to tack to cover or break cover, but this is always for tactical reasons and normally you want to do the best tack possible (although you may go in to footing or pinching mode later – see Chapter 4: Upwind Boatspeed).

The exact actions of a tack are, of course, dependent upon the class. A heavy keelboat may well maintain its speed very well, whereas a catamaran may lose its speed dramatically, and this will be reflected in the speed of the turn. Different classes of boat will have different optimum pointing angles (and top speeds) in different conditions.

A good run-to-run **gybe** follows the same principle: you need to continue to make maximum downwind progress. So the speed, and indeed turning angle, may vary widely from class to class as well as across the wind speed range.

A good reach-to-reach gybe is simply about getting the boat going as fast as possible in the new direction, as quickly as possible! When rounding a mark, a wide entry will allow a narrow exit so, assuming you have room, this is the preferred method. If it is extremely windy (and you are in safety mode) you may want to do a run-to-run gybe first, then head up slowly.

In both tacks and gybes there are really three points:

1. A slow smooth turn directly up or downwind: although the boat is slightly slowing, it is now pointing very close to the direction of the next mark (up or downwind).

2. A large roll when the boat is either head to wind or directly downwind: the amount of roll is dependent upon the class of boat and the wind strength.

3. The second half of the tack / gybe needs to be fast: rolling the boat flat, sheeting in and moving the crew weight to the normal racing position as soon as possible. Exiting the tack the rudder must be straight, so that it does not act as a brake.

Remember: the tack or gybe does not need to look pretty. It doesn't matter if you are not clipped onto the trapeze or whether you are holding the mainsheet hand right up in the air. As long as the boat trim / balance and sail setting is good, you will have good speed. You can worry about putting the tiller in the correct hand and tidying away the sheet later (as soon as you reach full speed).

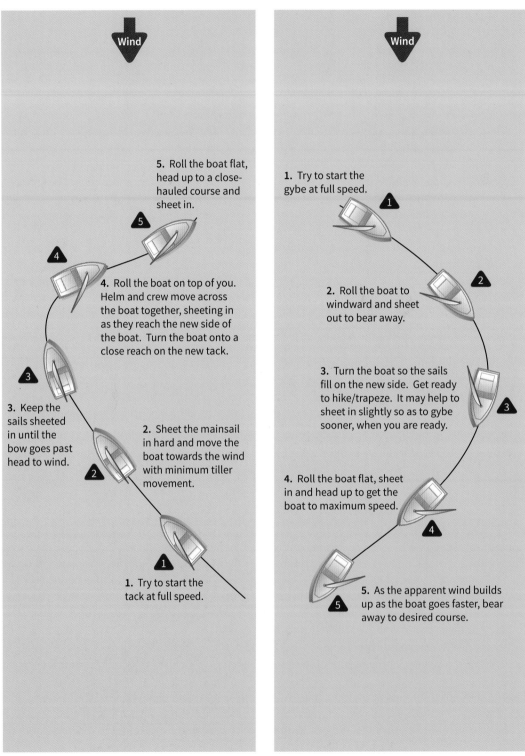

Wind

5. Roll the boat flat, head up to a close-hauled course and sheet in.

4. Roll the boat on top of you. Helm and crew move across the boat together, sheeting in as they reach the new side of the boat. Turn the boat onto a close reach on the new tack.

3. Keep the sails sheeted in until the bow goes past head to wind.

2. Sheet the mainsail in hard and move the boat towards the wind with minimum tiller movement.

1. Try to start the tack at full speed.

Wind

1. Try to start the gybe at full speed.

2. Roll the boat to windward and sheet out to bear away.

3. Turn the boat so the sails fill on the new side. Get ready to hike/trapeze. It may help to sheet in slightly so as to gybe sooner, when you are ready.

4. Roll the boat flat, sheet in and head up to get the boat to maximum speed.

5. As the apparent wind builds up as the boat goes faster, bear away to desired course.

Best course to sail when tacking *Best course to sail when gybing*

The best way to improve boat handling is with a series of exercises:

Exercise 1: Tacking

Have two boats line up upwind on converging tacks: one on port and one on starboard like a 'rabbit' start. The starboard boat ducks the port boat; both boats sail three boat lengths (vary according to class and wind strength – decrease time for slower boats and weaker winds) and then tack. When they come back together, both boats tack out again, sail for three boat lengths and then tack back. Continue until one boat is clearly ahead (can cross by two boat lengths). Now review the technique.

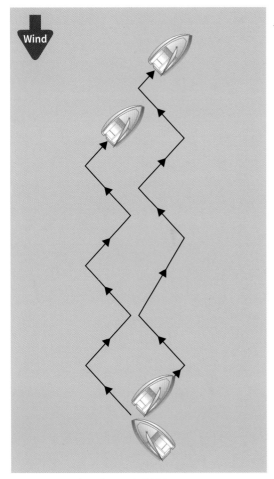

Exercise 1: Tacking from a 'rabbit' start

Exercise 2: Gybing

Start on a reach. On the count of three, sheet in and then tack round, bear away and then bear away onto a dead run. Now gybe (run-to-run) every 30 seconds (vary according to class and wind strength – increase time for faster boats and stronger winds). Continue for 20 gybes, but stop if a boat capsizes!

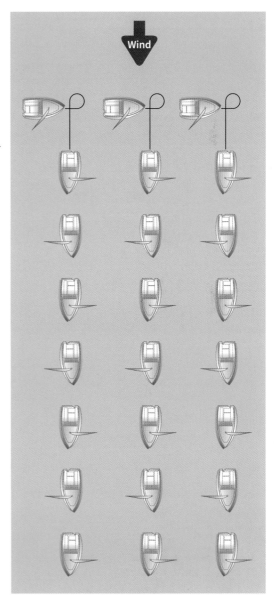

Exercise 2: Gybing every 30 seconds

Exercise 3: Downwind Slalom

Set up a slalom course. If you do not have a coach to set this up for you, try to find an area of moorings (without boats attached!). Try sailing 120 degrees from the wind, and gybing through 120 degrees. Where possible, do at least 10 gybes in a row. The closer together the marks are, the harder the exercise is. Try to do a racing turn (in wide, out tight) as well as doing a good gybe!

Exercise 4: Riverboat

Pretend you are sailing up a narrow river. This needs three points (ideally a coach boat and two buoys forming a start line) to make a triangle. You must stay within the triangle; you can call water at the sides. This means that those boats that end up at the front have to tack every few boat lengths to stay in the triangle (river).

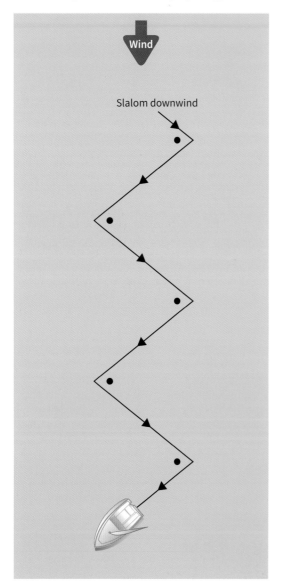

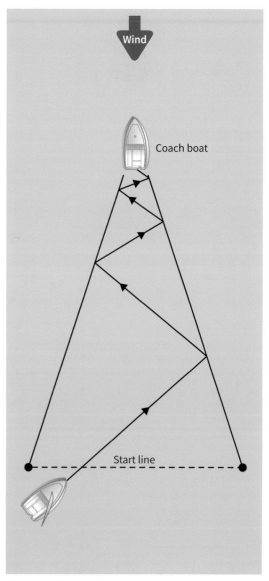

Exercise 3: Downwind slalom

Exercise 4: Riverboat

Exercise 5: Gut-buster

This is a windward / leeward course, with a short start line and a turning mark in the middle, called the gut-buster. You sail upwind from the start, around the turning mark, to the windward mark, then downwind around the turning mark and a hook finish through the gate. The shorter the course, the harder this is. Typically, each leg should be less than a minute to make it really hard. For boats with a spinnaker, this must be hoisted and dropped when going around the turning mark.

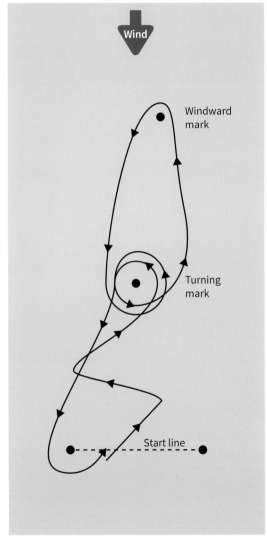

Exercise 5: Gut-buster

Changing Gear

Tacks and gybes actually have much in common: the movements of the hands and feet are to control the speed of the turn and the power in the boat. As the wind speed and rate of turn increase, these movements also increase and the exact movements of the hands and feet will remain similar. In light winds you need to use lots of roll to power through the turn, whereas in strong winds you need to move across the boat very quickly to control the power.

Wind speed	Boat handling type
Light winds	Lots of body movement and sheeting to push the boat through the tacks and gybes. (A bit of Elvis Presley: Rock and Roll!)
Medium winds	Continue to push the boat around the corners as 'hard' as you can. The key is to get the crew weight to the new side as soon as the power comes on.
Strong winds	Safety first – there is little benefit in pushing too hard. Highly focused steering and crew positioning are crucial. If necessary allow extra time to do the manoeuvres.

If the conditions of the day change, you not only need to adjust your rig for straight line speed but also to think about changing your boat handling. Sometimes (class dependent) it is not possible to change the rig during the race, so you may have to make large changes to your boat handling to compensate for being very over or underpowered.

The key area is transitions which may happen in a race. For example, in 25 knots you may 'tack as normal' whereas in a gust of 30 knots it may be sensible to do a 'safety tack'. Likewise if the wind drops you need to remember to use more roll in the middle part of the turn. Training in extreme conditions (very light or very windy) is an excellent way of improving boat handling and will of course make things seem much easier (when not sailing in extreme conditions).

Top & Bottom Turns in Waves

When sailing downwind you are always looking for the route of least resistance and this means looking for the gap in the waves, so that you can carry on surfing without loading up the rig by running into the bottom of the wave in front. The better the conditions, and the better the sailor, the more time you can spend surfing and often your speed is determined more by how many waves you miss than by how many you catch. Remember it takes far less energy to continue to surf than it does to get the boat to surf in the first place.

Even if it is possible to go over the waves, you are always looking for the lowest point to cross. When you start going over the waves you may start to jump clean over, so you need to be even more careful not to bury the bow in the wave in front, as hitting it at speed may lead to a pitchpole. At the point when you are going straight over the waves, you are now focusing on steering a straight line to the next mark, to minimise distance sailed (just like you would in non-surfing conditions).

When you need to steer over or to catch the waves good top and bottom turns become really important, especially in marginal surfing conditions. You need to position the crew weight perfectly so that the boat is finely balanced to go in one direction, but can be easily steered by a small change of bodyweight to windward or leeward.

By moving the body weight to leeward the shape of the boat encourages it to head up without having to use the rudder. When the boat is on its new course you can then roll the boat flat. This uses the energy of the crew to steer the boat rather than the rudder, which can slow it down.

To get the boat to head up, gently move the body weight to leeward

Similarly, by moving the body weight to windward the shape of the boat encourages the boat to bear away without having to use the rudder. When the boat is on its new (desired) course you can then move the weight in to flatten the boat.

When the boat is going in a straight line you should be able to let go of the tiller and the boat will continue in a straight line. Most classes of boat will sail fastest with minimum corrective steerage, as use of the rudder creates drag. So you steer the boat with body weight and sail setting rather than using the rudder.

When the boat is going in a straight line minimum rudder movement is required (here we see in a Laser the average leech position is approximately 90 degrees) on a dead run

TOP TIP

Your position fore and aft is dependent on the wind strength: the lighter the wind, the further forward you sit; the stronger the wind, the further back you sit.

The more kicker you have, the easier it is to make the boat head up but the harder it is to make it bear away and vice versa.

Advice from Olympic Gold Medallist (Laser class) Paul Goodison

" *Boat handling is the one area where everybody is capable of doing well; it is all about practice and keeping sharp.*

I try to break down each manoeuvre into several sections so that it is easier to analyse. For example, a leeward mark rounding would be split into entry, transition and exit. Each one of these areas can then be broken down further. It is important to master the first stage before trying to perfect the next stage, as an error early in the manoeuvre may affect the end.

There is no better way to train than just repeating the manoeuvres until they are perfect. Try to be very critical when things aren't quite right, and aim for perfection. Each small gain in boat handling leads to a much bigger gain on the race course; everybody will make small mistakes, so it's all about trying to minimise these errors. "

CHAPTER 3

Starting

Your finish position in a race is often heavily influenced by your start. With the tendency for major championships to move to more and shorter races, and with few discards, we cannot afford to have too many bad races: often it is the worst races that you count in your series, not the best, which decide your overall position. So consistency is key, and making a good start can really help to get consistent results.

Position, Speed & Time

Obviously in some races the start will be more important, perhaps when one side of the course is heavily favoured, and less important in others, perhaps when the course is even and you are fast in the conditions, but, without a doubt, the ability to start well is a championship winning requirement.

Starting is a skill and, as with any skill, practice makes perfect! If you always practise starting at the pin end you will most likely get very good at it, but you may struggle when you need to start at the starboard end. You also need to make the practice as specific as possible. Starting in a Nacra 17 is very different from starting in a Laser. So one of the first skills to learn in a new class is how to get a good start.

A good start requires three elements:

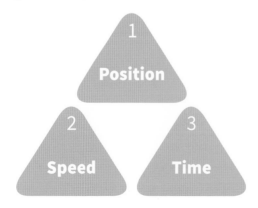

If any of these elements are missing, then you won't have a good start:

- If you start at the right time and have good speed but you are in the wrong position (unfavoured end of the line) then you have a poor start (everyone at the favoured end has a large advantage over you).
- If you start at the right time and in the right position (favoured end of the line) but you are not at full speed then you have a poor start (the boats at full speed will quickly pass you and give you dirty wind).
- If you start at the right position (favoured end of the line) and at good speed but your timing is wrong then you have a poor start (2 seconds early and you are clearly OCS, 2 seconds late and everyone is already in front of you giving you dirty wind).

Often it is only obvious 30 seconds after the start whether your start was good. Think, "Do I have clean wind, good speed and am I going in the direction that I want to?". Both good boat handling (see Chapter 2) and good upwind boatspeed (see Chapter 4) are required for a good start.

1. Position
We need to ask ourselves: "How easy is it to sit on the line?"; "How far will we drift forward / backward / to leeward?". Remember, you need space to leeward to accelerate into but you have

to avoid boats to leeward, as you don't want to be taking a penalty at start time.

Exercise 1: **Position**

Find a buoy. Start as close as you can, either with the mark to windward or leeward, and hold position for as long as possible.

Buoy to Windward

Start right next to the buoy; the boat will slowly drift to leeward (the exact speed depending upon the conditions). When you are two boat lengths from the buoy, put in two tacks and start again. To tack without going over the line, sheet in as little as possible to get the boat moving, overemphasise the steering and, if possible, back the main by pushing the boom out when you pass, head to wind. (This will stop you going forwards, as well as helping you turn.) To get the bow down, back the jib by pulling in the 'wrong' sheet. With a self-tacking jib, literally pull it to windward.

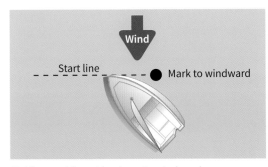

Holding position with a buoy to windward

Buoy to Leeward

Start two boat lengths from the buoy and stay on the line for as long as possible. Once you get to the point where you can no longer sail over the line (do not hit the buoy!), reverse out, and sail back to your original starting position without crossing the line.

To reverse, put the boat head to wind and push the boom as far forward as it will go. Remember, as you start to go backwards you have no rights and the steering will be acting in reverse!

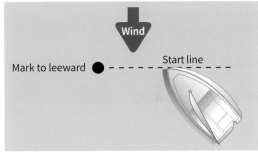

Holding position with a buoy to leeward

> **TOP TIP**
>
> **Keep the boat flat to stop it going sideways. (If, for some reason, you wish to go sideways, simply lift the centreboard.) If you end up going head to wind, release some kicker. When you go backwards you need to keep the weight well forward to stop the transom from digging in.**

2. Speed

Now we have looked at position, we can look at speed: specifically the time it takes to get to top speed. The time to accelerate a boat will, of course, depend upon the class of boat, but all boats accelerate best around their 'designed wind'. This is usually medium airs (around 14 knots), with high performance boats getting powered up sooner than lower performance boats. In these conditions, the sails are fully powered up, but the boat is not overpowered (so crew weight obviously has an impact here). If the breeze is noticeably lighter or stronger than this, the boat will be less efficient and so will take longer to get up to full speed for the conditions. A good starting point would be to tune the boat for accelerating in medium airs, then adjusting it for the specific conditions of the day.

Exercise 2: Speed

A great exercise to practise acceleration involves three identical boats (with sailors of similar ability). They line up, completely stationary (perhaps as you would be ten seconds before the start – depending upon your class). All boats are an equal distance apart and the closer the boats are together, the harder the exercise becomes. The boat in the middle then shouts loudly, "3, 2, 1, Go!".

Only on the "go" can the sailors start to move the boats forward (no cheating!). As soon as one boat clearly ends up ahead, or one boat clearly ends up behind, stop, and repeat the exercise. It is also worth doing this exercise on both tacks (even though you will usually start on starboard, being able to accelerate a boat is an extremely useful skill in itself!). You need to change the middle

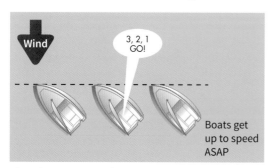

Three boat trigger pulling

boat each time, so the leeward boat becomes the middle boat, the middle boat becomes the windward boat and the windward boat becomes the leeward boat.

> ### TOP TIP
>
> To help the boat get up to pace, you need to bear away. Get the boat to bear away without going forward (by using the rudder but not allowing the sail to fill), so the boat does not go over the start line, but is in a good position to accelerate easily. This is often referred to as 'getting the bow down'.

When setting up the rig, it may pay to have slightly more power than you would normally need upwind for the conditions, so that you can keep your height and do not fall into the boat to leeward of you. This also helps if the wind and waves are very disturbed around the starting area. In addition you should be able to hike / trapeze really hard for the first minute or so of the race, to get the edge on your competition.

3. Time

In an ideal world you will hit the line at full speed. You need to know how much time this will take so that you are in the correct position at start time. The class of boat will make a big difference, but so will the conditions. However, remember both the wind and the water are likely to be confused around the starting area, so it may well take more distance than you think to get up to full speed.

Exercise 3: Time

On your own, start next to a buoy, and from stationary see how long it takes you to get up to full speed. Now go back to the line and start the same distance back. See if you have the distance about right.

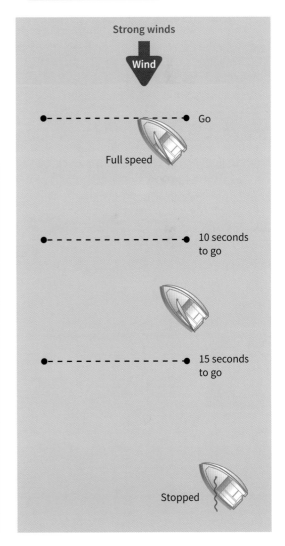

Timed run

Identifying the Favoured End

When considering your start, remember that the closer you are to the favoured end, the greater your advantage (regardless of what is causing that advantage), but also the more crowded this part of the line is likely to be. If you are over, it is easy to go round the ends. However, in a black flag situation you need to be especially careful, as you are going to be more likely to have your numbers recorded.

It is also possible that the favoured end of the line may not be the favoured side of the beat (for example, you may start at the port end and wish to go right, or start at the starboard end and go left). If you are not confident about getting a good start and going the best way up the beat, you need to consider which is the more important factor.

But first let us look at the factors that determine which is the favoured end of the start line.

Wind

Assuming that the wind remains constant in strength and direction, and there is no current or difference in the waves, the favoured end of the line is the part which is most upwind.

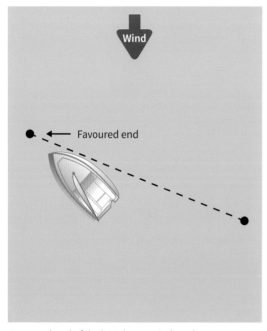

Favoured end of the line due to wind angle

The simplest method to identify this is to go head to wind on the line and see which end of the line you are pointing closest to. This is much better than sailing up and down the line, which may be difficult to do accurately, complicated by the presence of other boats and, with a large line, may well take some time.

In reality, the wind is often oscillating, which means that the favoured end of the line may continually change. In this case you do not want to commit yourself to starting at one end of the line too early. (With a long line you may not be able to get down to the new favoured end if there is a large wind shift.) If there is a regular pattern you may well be able to predict what the wind is going to do at / shortly before / shortly after start time. (Try to get to the starting area early and track what the wind is doing.)

Please note that if the windward mark is slightly offset to the left or right, this in no way affects the line bias; it simply means that you will spend more time on one tack than the other!

There could also be a difference in wind strength across the course, resulting in one side being favoured, perhaps due to wind funnelling around a landmass.

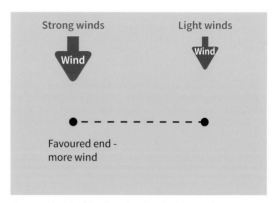

Favoured end of the line due to wind strength

If a mark is the favoured end of the start line (as it is the mark most to windward) then it is also the favoured mark to round as a downwind gate (as this mark and the windward mark are closer to each other than the other end of the line and the windward mark).

Current

Over the course of a day the tide will no doubt vary considerably. For example, the current may have no effect on the first race of the day, when the wind is strong and the current is weak, but at the end of the day the current may be the most important factor, when the wind has dropped and the current has increased. You should look at the predicted current flows for a regatta before you even drive to the venue!

If the line is square to the wind, you want to start at the end with the most favourable current (being careful not to be over) or the least adverse current (remembering that it will be harder to hold your position on the line).

If the current is flowing parallel to the line it makes no difference to the line bias. However, the end of the line the current is flowing to is likely to be very crowded so, if everything else is equal, you should aim to start at the other end (up current). If the current is strong, boats at the extreme ends may not be able to get across the line.

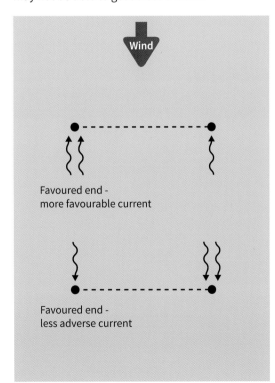

Favoured end of the line due to current

If the water changes depth across the race course, current may be significant, for example at the top of the beat, when it did not matter at the bottom of the beat.

Other Factors

If the wind and current are equal across the race course, but there are differences in waves, head for the area where you can sail fastest. To sail faster upwind try to sail in flat water. Downwind, if you can surf (in a Laser, for example), the waves may help you sail faster. However, if you are planing freely (for example, in a 49er), waves will slow you down and you should avoid them.

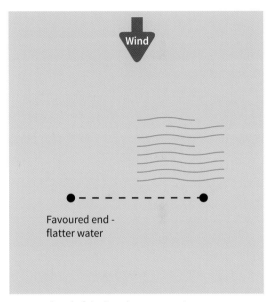

Favoured end of the line due to wave size

In Summary

You need to weigh up the current conditions (and future predictions) when choosing where to start on the line. Remember, being a small way down from the favoured end will probably make it easier to find some space to accelerate into.

After the race, try to sit down and work out whether you feel you made the correct decision – and always try to learn from your mistakes! You will find that you will visit some venues repeatedly, and that the race area, dates of the regatta and start times may well be similar.

Different Places to Start

The Middle

The most difficult place to start is probably in the very middle of the line, as here it is hardest to know whether you are on the line. This accounts for the common mid-line sag.

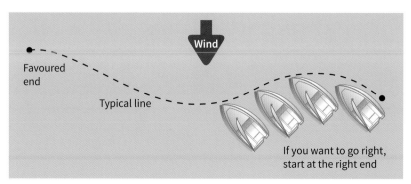

Middle line sag

What you really need is some transits: two objects lined up that tell you whether you are on the line or not. If you are confident in your position you may even be able to start on port! Transits may be taken from in front or behind, and need to be two large and immoveable objects.

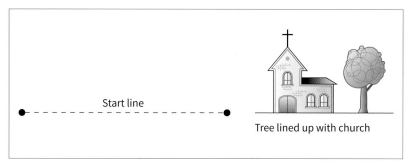

Transits

Exercise 4: Transits

A powerboat is anchored and the sailors sail up to the middle of the line (the longer the line, the harder the exercise). When, and only when, the boat is stationary, the sailors raise a hand and the person on the powerboat can then inform them whether they are on / over / behind the line. Ideally, the exercise is repeated until the sailors are consistently on the line.

Port / Pin End

When you start at the port / pin end you need to be careful. If you start right by the buoy it is possible that you may not be able to get over the line at all.

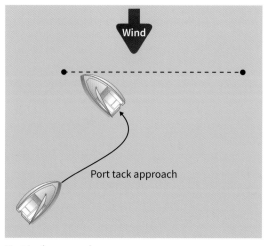

Port tack approach

The best way is often to come in from port on port and find a natural gap along the line. Look at how the line is building and time your approach accordingly. If you have to duck boats, being on port is an advantage as the other boats on starboard will be moving slightly, so you will pass more boats than you would if you had to sail under them on starboard.

Starboard / Committee Boat End

Starting at the starboard end may be quite difficult. Often a large committee boat will have a large wind shadow, and, if you are over, you are likely to get your number taken.

You will need to choose early on how close to the committee boat you wish to start. Often this is dictated by how soon you wish to tack after the start. (If you want to go right you may even consider risking a second row start right by the committee boat if it guarantees that you will be among the first to tack!)

See how quickly you drift sideways and line up so that you will be where you wish to be at the start time. Quality fleets may line up quite early, and there is unlikely to be much room if the line is quite biased. Think: is it a day when a gap is likely to appear?

> ### TOP TIP
>
> The more kicker you have on, the more the boat will want to go head to wind. The more kicker you let off, the more the boat will slip sideways. Try to find a balance point, which is usually about halfway between kicker fully off and the kicker you will be using on the beat.
>
> If you do lose your space, try to look for another one early – if there is still time. Sometimes you will be forced to start in a difficult place, but often there is a better alternative (even if not absolutely ideal).
>
> Once you are completely stationary or head to wind, it is very hard to manoeuvre, so avoid this if possible.

The Final Moments

Ready

Keeping your gap to leeward is vital: you need the space to accelerate into. When everyone is looking for a space to start, you need to protect your gap ('shutting the door'). Keep the bow off the wind (below a close-hauled course); the boom is now out (the sails are flapping) – which closes the gap. If any sailors come in to leeward, they must give you room to keep clear. As you head up to avoid them you will still have room (although the hole will now be smaller). To create space, or to make it larger, work the boat up to above a close-hauled course (without sheeting in the sails).

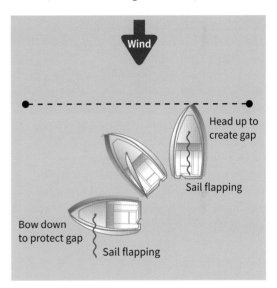

Protecting the gap

Steady

For the start, make any final rig changes before you bear away. Use the jib to help you do this before the gun and go down to below a close-hauled course, allowing your sails to fill on a close reach. (As soon as the boat is up to speed you may return to a close-hauled course.) If you do not have a jib, you will need to use the rudder to bear away. Pull the tiller towards you hard, gently push it away and then pull it hard towards you again. Ensure that the bow is bearing away and you are not making the boat go forward (as this would break Rule 42).

Go!

Whatever happens, as soon as the gun has gone, concentrate on getting your boat up to maximum speed. Now 'get your head out of the boat' to consider your options (carry on or tack) as these early decisions will make a big impact on your race – and remember, keep trying!

Sailing is a dynamic sport and it is possible to recover from a poor start. It is often these races (not your best ones) which decide the outcome of a championship. You can discuss what went wrong (or right!) with the start after the race. Keeping good records is vital. You may even choose to use a regatta as a 'practice regatta', so as to test your starts – often two OCSs in a regatta could be disastrous.

Remember the Final Result

The start is the beginning of the race, not the end. A good start certainly makes it easier to have a good race, and a bad start certainly makes it harder, but the final result is never decided until you cross the finishing line (or hear the facts found at a protest hearing!).

So it is important to see the big picture: there is no point winning the port end of the line if you miss the first shift because you cannot tack.

When lots of boats are being OCSed, a more cautious approach may be advisable as you need to consider whether it is worth the risk lining up where other boats are very close to, or even over, the line, especially early on in the series where an OCS could affect the way you race for the rest of the event. Often it may be obvious when a race is likely to be general recalled; this is not the time to push the line hard!

When looking at the start you must consider the first beat. If one side of the race course is heavily biased, due to differences in wind speed (more wind) or angle (a wind bend) or current differences, it may well be worth considering starting away from what you would consider the favoured end of the line to ensure that you can work the favoured side of the beat!

TOP TIP

Even when you know your boat and a venue very well it is always sensible to go out early to check your equipment, your boatspeed and to allow you to be relaxed properly and focused for the race (arriving at the race course late can cause a whole host of problems).

By doing the first beat and then coming back downwind you can be happy with your boatspeed (and rig set up) as well as knowing, for example, that your spinnaker is easy to hoist and drop. Give yourself plenty of time to rectify any mistakes that you may come across.

Advice from Olympic Gold Medallist (Laser class) Paul Goodison

- *Become comfortable with the conditions. I sail most of the beat before the start sequence to gain confidence in my boatspeed and set up.*

- *Devise a plan and strategy: which way do I want to go up the beat?*

- *Where do I want to start?*

- *Once the line is set, look for transits and decide how valuable they might be.*

- *Once the warning signal has sounded, it's time to double check the transit and line bias.*

- *Get ready to synchronise the watch at the preparatory signal.*

- *Sail upwind again to double check the set up and the line bias.*

- *Leaving the sail controls set in the upwind settings but with the kicker eased, return behind the line. Leaving the kicker eased stops the boat from accelerating when hovering.*

- *At the 1 minute signal, check the timing again and get in position for the final approach. This may need to be done earlier in larger fleets when the line is heavily biased.*

- *Try to maintain sight of one end of the line at all times, so as to be able to gauge your position.*

- *You need to be aware of what is happening around, especially boats entering from astern that may steal the gap to leeward.*

- *With 25 seconds to go, start to create a gap to leeward. Any earlier than this and the gap will be open for others.*

- *With 10 seconds to go, pull the kicker on and start to pull the bow down to accelerate.*

- *With 3 seconds to go, the boat should be up to speed ready to hit the line with pace.*

- *When accelerating, bring the bow down below close-hauled as this will help to accelerate, and create flow around the foils, which stops the boat slipping sideways.*

- *The first 30 seconds after the start are the most critical. All concentration should be on boatspeed and holding the lane. Don't look round or fiddle with controls until advanced on the boats around.*

- *The key to good starts is confidence in your ability and confidence in where the line is, so you can attack it flat out knowing that you are not over.*

CHAPTER 4

Upwind Boatspeed

It has often been said that upwind boatspeed makes you a tactical genius; it gives you the option to go where you want to go on the race course, so paying attention to your speed can make a huge difference to your end result.

In conditions where you know that you are fast, it means that you could make a more conservative start and it could allow you to tack close to someone, knowing that you are unlikely to be rolled or lee bowed. Although being fast upwind will not guarantee that you win races, being slow can make it nearly impossible to win.

Crew Weight & Equipment

Correct crew weight, selection of equipment and rig set up are essential.

Crew Weight

A crew weight that may be a clear advantage in one condition may be a real disadvantage in another, so it is crucial that you are a competitive weight throughout the expected wind range (it may be worth adjusting your weight to suit your usual conditions – so lighter for small inland waters surrounded by trees and heavier for venues with strong reliable thermal winds). Crew weight will, of course, affect the class you choose to sail (or maybe just the person you sail with for a particular series!).

Choosing your Equipment

It is important that you use good quality equipment. If you are not sure which equipment to use, then try using that used by the current National Champion and / or the majority of the fleet. This will be a good starting point and you are likely to be able to get lots of help and advice. You can worry later about getting that extra edge through equipment development.

The more that you know and understand about your equipment (and the more adjustable or wider range of equipment that you have) the better. This means that you can perform not only at your usual venue, but also at other venues as well and, of course, at big events, often the wind will seem to be very different from how it normally is!

Rig Set Up

The good thing about rig set up is that you can adjust it, which is just as well, as a set up which may be great for medium conditions when you are searching for power, could be very slow when another 15 knots arrive! Also remember a fast set up for some sailors may not be fast for you if you have different equipment, different crew weights or just a different sailing style.

The rake settings for your class are usually available through your class association. When you are racing you need to ensure that you 'get your head out of the boat' and are not purely focused on adjusting your equipment, as accurate steering, sheeting and body movements make a big difference to speed and you also need to see the big picture: the strategic and tactical considerations.

Upwind maximum power is achieved when the mast bend matches the luff curve of the sail. These measurements should be obtainable from your sail maker and mast manufacturer. Even small differences can lead to a difference in performance.

You may not have a huge range of equipment (soft mast, hard mast, full sails, flat sails, etc.) so it is important that you know how to optimise what you do have for different conditions, and it is not always possible to adjust everything.

The Kicking Strap

A good example of this is a boat with an unstayed mast, like the Laser, where the kicker has many effects: mast bend, sail fullness, centre of effort in the sail, leech tension – making it a very important sail control indeed.

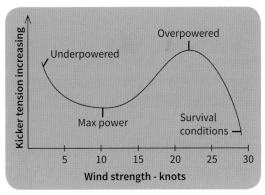

Increasing kicker tension bends the mast, flattens the sail and decreases power

The Centre of Effort

The rig set up not only controls the shape and power of the sail (by adjusting the fullness of the sail and the leech tension) but the rake of rig also affects the centre of effort of the sail. The further forward this is the easier it is to foot, and the further back it is the easier it is to pinch.

It should be noted that, in most conditions, it is fastest to keep the centre of effort over the centre of resistance (which can also be adjusted by raking the centreboard and moving the crew) to ensure minimum corrective steering. After all if you are using the rudder to 'force' the boat to continue to sail in a straight line then it is acting as a brake.

A good example of when the centre of effort is too far back would be a single-sailed boat where there is a lot of leech tension (and little luff tension in the sail) and the boat keeps on wanting to head up into the wind. This effect, where the tiller

extension keeps trying to pull itself out of your hand (especially in the gusts), is called weather helm (you keep having to pull the helm to weather).

An example of when the centre of effort is too far forward would be in a spinnaker boat where there is a huge amount of sail area in front of the mast (perhaps on a bow sprit) and the boat keeps on wanting to bear away. The effect, where the tiller extension needs to be pushed hard (especially in the gusts) just to go in a straight line, is called lee helm (you keep having to push the helm to leeward).

Centre of effort behind centre of resistance

Move crew and centreboard forward. Rake rig back.

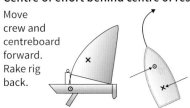

Centre of effort behind centre of resistance = boat wants to head up.

Centre of effort in front of centre of resistance

Move crew and centreboard back. Rake rig forward.

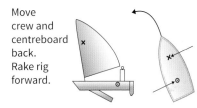

Centre of effort in front of centre of resistance = boat wants to bear away.

Centre of effort over centre of resistance

Centre of effort over centre of resistance = boat wants to go in a straight line.

✕ Centre of effort is around the draft (deepest / most powerful point) of the sails. This has some force to leeward as well as driving the boat forward.

⊙ Centre of resistance is around the crew weight and last edge of the centreboard and this opposes the forces driving the boat to leeward.

⍟ Crew.

Looking at the effect of centre of effort and centre of resistance

Adjusting the Settings

When the conditions are constantly changing, you need to constantly change the rig so that it is always optimised for the conditions. Of course, if the conditions are constant, then there is no need to make adjustments, but this is rarely the case. If there are big changes in the conditions (very gusty, very shifty, etc.) then you need to set the rig up to make the boat 'easy to sail'.

It is not only the wind which affects how you set up the boat, the waves have an impact too:

Water state	Sails	Effect
Flat water	Flat sails	Less power Less drag
Choppy water	Fuller sails	More power More acceleration
Flat water	Tight leech	Harder to steer Better pointing
Choppy water	Looser leech	Easy to steer Better speed

Steering & Crew Positioning

Steering

Even the way you steer the boat changes with the waves. So if the wave height is small, then the size of the turn is small (and if the wave height is large, then the size of the turn is large). Likewise if the wave frequency is high (choppy water) then the steering reflects this and vice versa. The choppier the waves the choppier the steering needs to be, and the smoother the waves the smoother the steering can be. Finally, remember that the sheeting will also match the steering (so when you do big steering movements you need to do big sheeting adjustments and so on).

The aim of steering upwind is simple: to avoid hitting the waves and maximise water line length in boats which do not plane. Generally, if you feel you are fighting the boat, it is not a good sign. You need to listen to what the boat is trying to tell you. If you keep putting the bow of the boat into the waves then you are not heading up enough or your crew weight / mast rake is too far forward. If you

find the bow is being blown 'off the water' (you are struggling for height rather than speed) then you have the opposite issue to resolve.

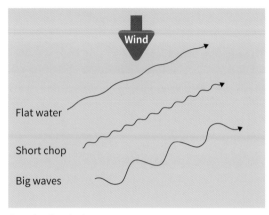

Steering in relation to waves

Crew Positioning

Sailing is a dynamic sport; things are always changing. Not only do you need to move the crew weight in and out to balance the boat windward / leeward, but small movements fore and aft help to maximise speed. It is not simply finding the correct place to sit and staying there. Indeed, if you find you keep leaning backwards, then you are probably sitting too far forwards, and vice versa. In medium to strong winds those crews who work the hardest will be amongst the fastest, but however powerful the movements required, precision and timing are crucial. Sheeting or steering at the wrong time can sometimes be far worse than doing nothing.

The crew weight needs to be roughly in the middle of the boat, making it easy to make small movements forward and backward in response to the waves

Making the Boat 'Point'

It is, of course, impossible to sail head to wind, but a boat can make good progress to windward if set up correctly at a variety of angles. When you sail as close to the wind as possible, whilst maintaining maximum VMG (Velocity Made Good) to the next mark, we refer to this as pointing. You may be going slower than other boats but you will be reducing the distance you need to sail to reach the windward mark.

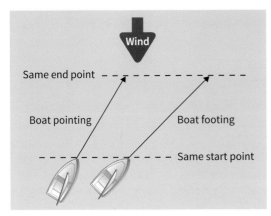

Both the boat pointing and the boat footing travel exactly the same distance directly upwind and will reach the windward mark at precisely the same time (they are both maximising their VMG)

Being able to point high can have huge tactical advantages: for example, in race strategy you may be able to stay on the lifting tack whilst minimising your progress into stronger adverse currents, or it may be the difference between having the current on your lee bow (and therefore helping you to windward) or on your windward bow (forcing you to leeward). Tactically, being able to sail high may help you keep your lane off the start line and make it easier to lee bow other boats and be less likely to be lee bowed yourself.

To point high (pinch) you need to maximise the power effectively (assuming that you are not overpowered). This means powering up the rig and maybe even moving the crew weight inboard (although be careful not to allow your speed to drop too much).

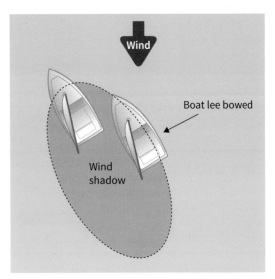

The lee bow

You also need a tight leech, usually through mainsheet tension, to 'foot off', and avoid the use of the cunningham where possible (as this not only opens the upper leech but pulls the draft of the sail forward).

A flat boat, with a tight leech and powered up sails, provides maximum pointing ability

Obviously, in terms of boat balance, you need to keep the boat flat to minimise leeway and in some classes it may be possible to heel the boat to windward to actually gain height. It may also be worth moving the crew weight slightly further forward than normal, so ensure that the bow is 'in the water' at all times (although move back if you start slowing significantly).

It takes far more energy to accelerate a boat rather than to keep it at speed, so work hard to keep your average speed up. If you start to slow, do something about it quickly, rather than waiting until it is a big problem. It is like running a 10 kilometre race: it is far more efficient to run it at 10 km 'pace' than to sprint at 100 metre pace, then walk for 900 metres, then sprint 100 metres again...

Making the Boat 'Foot'

Leech twist makes it easier to bear the boat away and maximise speed

Maximising the VMG to windward, whilst sailing low, is called footing, so this means that the boat really is at top speed. As a result it is less likely to be affected by bad waves, etc., as the average speed is higher. So putting the bow down can work really well in short chop. Also when the boat is going fast there tends to be better flow over the foils, making them work more effectively and reducing leeway. So in some conditions it can really pay to foot!

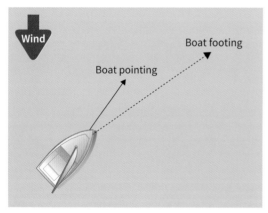

Better progress to the windward mark can be made by footing

Just like pointing, there are some times when sacrificing height for speed can have some clear strategic advantages: like getting into the new shift / more pressure / better current first, as well as tactical advantages. You can quickly get to the same side of the race course as your main rivals or even roll over the top of them, giving them dirty wind (or quickly escape dirty wind if someone is trying to cover you).

Advice from Double Olympic Medallist (470 class) Joe Glanfield

" *A lot of upwind boatspeed in technical boats comes from good consistent settings. Normally nothing special, but a question of having your boat well calibrated so that you are able to put the controls in the right place for the right condition, and then repeat it the next day.*

To transfer this onto a race course, good communication (on a double-handed boat) is key, especially when the wind is inconsistent. It needs to be one sailor's responsibility to call the gusts and lulls so that the other sailor can adjust the controls to match. Often sailors struggle to transfer tuning speed to the race course. This is normally because both sailors are looking around too much whilst racing, when actually just one sailor could do the majority of looking around whilst the other concentrates on the boatspeed.

In our boat I concentrated on the tactics so that Nick never had to look outside the boat and could just focus on steering and sail settings. I believe that the communication between me and Nick, and our clearly defined roles in the boat, were some of the main reasons why we were fast across the wind range. "

CHAPTER 5

Reaching Boatspeed

For many people, reaching is the most fun point of sailing and it is another great opportunity to gain places during a race.

Rig Set Up

The rig changes from upwind to reaching need to be done as quickly and as efficiently as possible to keep the boat going at maximum possible speed at all times. However, give yourself as long as you need to make the changes on strong wind or big wave days.

The exact rig changes will depend upon the conditions of the day (for example more power in moderate conditions, less power when it is very windy) and the angle of the next leg of the course. If the angle (for whatever reason) is similar to a beat, then the rig set up will be similar to a beat; if the angle is nearly a run, then the rig set up will be similar to a run. Remember the wind direction may have changed since you did the previous lap, or the marks may have been reset (or alternative marks put in their place), if the wind had shifted.

If you want to go 'low' on a leg you may be wanting to put as much power in the rig as possible (without creating drag), but if you want to keep your height in overpowered conditions you may need to keep the sails flatter. All of these considerations need to be thought of well in advance of arriving at the windward mark.

Perhaps the key control is the kicker, as leech tension will determine how easy it is to bear away. Indeed, in some classes it may be physically impossible to bear away with the kicker in its normal upwind setting for the conditions of the day.

When sailing downwind, the more kicker you have the more the boat will want to head up (it

will be easier to head up and will be harder to bear away) and vice versa. This is because letting the kicker off opens the leech (meaning that you are less likely to head up accidentally in the gusts) and it also brings the centre of effort forward in the boat, making it easier to bear away.

For this reason letting the kicker off before a gybe is often advisable, as it makes it easier to bear away and is therefore more likely to be a good gybe. Letting the kicker off also raises the boom height: often, if the boom is too low, it can hit the water on the exit of the gybe which results in a capsize (when the boom hits a wave it often looks as if the boat trips over it, as the sail gets sheeted in by the forward motion of the boat pulling the boom in – and of course you cannot let the boom out as the water holds it firmly in place).

Boat Trim

Boat trim is also adjusted, just like the rig set up, according to wind strength and wave height. Generally, the higher the waves the more the crew weight needs to be moved forward and back for any given wind strength to keep the trim perfect. In light winds you need to try to keep the maximum wetted surface area, which often means keeping the weight well forward and having a smooth flow of water leaving the transom. In stronger winds, however, when you can plane, you need to get the bow lifted as early as possible and then move as far back in the boat as possible whilst maintaining the smooth flow of water off the transom. Sometimes when it is really windy and wavy you cannot get far enough back in the boat!!!

'Soaking' Low

'Soaking' is a term used to describe getting the boat to go as low as possible without losing too much speed, to keep your maximum VMG to the next mark. You may need to do this for tactical reasons, to gain an overlap at the next mark, or for strategic reasons like staying in the pressure of good tide. It may even pay to soak below the layline if you know the wind and tide are going to change during the course of the leg.

This is all about feel: you need to feel how the boat behaves by gently bearing the boat away until the point you know that, if you go any further, you will start to lose speed. As soon as you start to lose speed (or ideally before this point) you need to come back up again. This not only means being sensitive to changes in wind speed and direction, but also getting your head out of the boat, to see what to expect and to communicate this to the rest of the crew.

Remember it is far more efficient to keep the average speed up rather than to keep slowing down and speeding up all the time.

You need to ensure that, when you go low, you are going to have clean breeze. There is no point going slightly low only to be passed to windward by the boats who immediately take your wind. You really need to be about six mast heights to leeward for the boats to have no effect on you but, the greater the separation, the safer you are.

When initially bearing away try to do so using the crew weight to roll to windward to drive the turn rather than using excess rudder. When you are on the desired course you can flatten the boat to keep it going in the new target direction using minimum corrective steering. This is true for any change of angle: try to use body weight and sheeting to drive the turns and just let the rudder 'follow' the boat.

Use your turning of the boat to maximise average speed by spending as much time in the stronger winds as possible and then allow the boat to head back up in the lulls. This may mean that you do a huge number of small turns, so you have to be very focused.

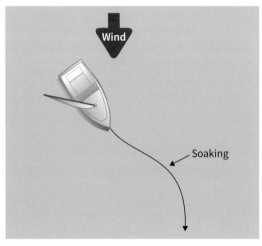

Soaking

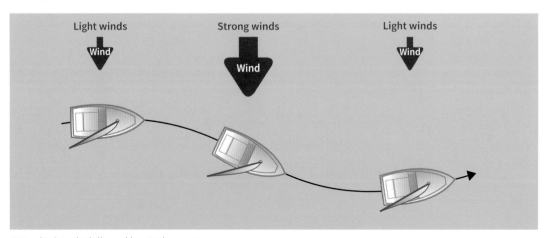

Going high in the lulls and low in the gusts

Going for Speed

For either tactical or strategic reasons you may want to go high and fast; perhaps to roll over another boat and take her wind (tactical) or maybe just to get into an area of stronger wind or out of adverse tide (strategic considerations). Whatever the reason, you need to be prepared and to set the boat up accordingly (one of the big decisions may be whether to hoist the spinnaker or not).

It is usually easier to sail fast when you are 'on your own'. There are two reasons for this:
1. Psychologically: it is easier to focus without other boats in close proximity to you.
2. Physically: boats will go faster when their wind and water is not disturbed by other boats.

These are two common reasons why the leaders often get well clear of the fleet.

Again you must really listen to what the boat is telling you. You will feel when you are trying to push the boat too high and are losing VMG. As soon as you get to the point where you head up and the boatspeed isn't increasing you know that you have gone too far. Bear away to the point of maximum boatspeed. Then you know you have reached the optimum angle.

As the wind speed and boatspeed change, the optimum angle will change too. The faster you go the more apparent wind you have and the more you need to sheet in to hold the same course. You may even need to bear away to keep the sails full.

When it is time to gybe you need to remember that you will have a bigger turning angle than you would if going slow. Therefore you may want to bear away slightly towards an average course before you go for the gybe. Remember to pay close attention to the Racing Rules as, if you are going at high speed, then the closing speeds can be amazing.

The secret is to be in tune with the boat. Often this (good boatspeed) happens when you are sailing on a subconscious level, relaxed but focused at the same time. This comes with experience (experience of the boat, experience of the venue, experience of the conditions). It is, of course, much harder to make the boat go fast when you feel stressed and under pressure, but actually everyone feels like this to some extent at regattas which are important to them.

Practice makes perfect: doing long tuning runs is the best way to learn and remember fast techniques as it builds 'muscle memory'. Sail for 20 minutes or more to get really happy with the fastest set up and then try to analyse your performance afterwards to get the best possible VMG (see overleaf).

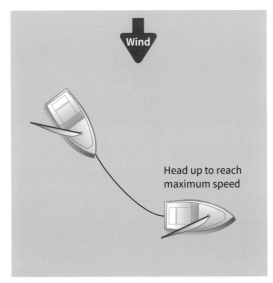

Steering for speed

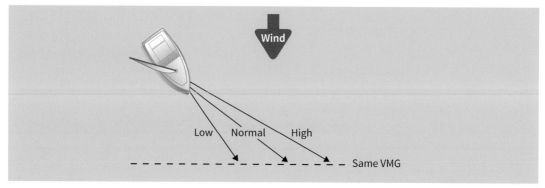

Three courses maximising VMG

Advice from Double Olympic Medallist (49er class) Simon Hiscocks

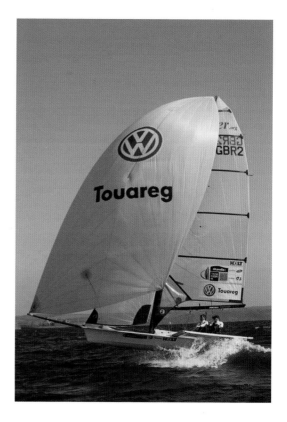

" *Due to the normal course configurations, asymmetric skiffs rarely reach. It could be argued that skiffs always reach downwind, which is a reasonable assumption. Let us consider what is happening between a boat trying to sail low and one that is trying to sail high to lay a mark (i.e. a proper reach and an apparent wind downwind run).*

Wind is wind, so whether it is true wind or apparent wind it still has the same effect of an air mass hitting a boat's rig at a given wind speed. Therefore, if a boat goes faster, it gets more wind. Lightweight skiffs tend to sail fastest on a run by sailing as fast as possible. This creates more wind (air mass hitting the boat) and the effect is better VMG.

Conversely, if the boat is sailing higher than is required, slowing it down will reduce the amount of wind that hits the boat's rig. Less wind will mean less power, so the boat can sail closer to the wind. The closer to the wind the boat sails, the slower it will go. This means that it's possible to slow down by sailing closer to the wind. Of course, there is a limit to this. Taken to an extreme, the boat either capsizes or ends up head to wind. Hence, there is a fine line when trying to sail too high with the kite up.

Keeping all the sails well eased will help reduce power. And, depending on how secure the mast is, pulling on the cunningham will also help. (The 49er mast is not secure enough for this!) Over easing the kite has the effect of folding the luff back on itself, which helps to reduce power, but it does need a fair bit

of sheeting in and out to control. Lastly, keep as much weight out as possible to create maximum leverage, and slow down by heading up to create leeward heel. Be careful of the rudder stalling. If and when it does stall, flow can be reattached by straightening the rudder angle to the centre line. This might feel a bit odd as it will probably feel like heading up. Dumping the kite will also help. Good communication between helm and crew is essential. "

CHAPTER 6

Running Boatspeed

Gone are the days when the downwind leg was a chance for a quick rest! Indeed, in some classes of boat, the downwind legs can be far more physically demanding than the upwind legs, and there is always an opportunity to overtake boats or extend your lead. Races are often finished at, or relatively close to, the leeward mark, so downwind speed is now far more important than in the days of long beats to the finish line.

Rig Set Up

Just like any other leg of the course, the correct rig set up is vital to achieve maximum boatspeed on the run. You need to achieve a balance so that the boat wants to go fast in a straight line (requiring minimal corrective steering) rather than wanting to head up or bear away all the time, but you also want to be able to use the crew weight to change course easily to take advantage of pressure and waves.

When going in a straight line the boat balance needs to be stable. You don't want to waste the wind's energy heeling the boat to leeward (in a gust) or to windward (in a lull); you want all the force driving you forwards, which means a well tuned rig and a responsive crew (moving their weight a lot so that the boat balance and trim stay optimal).

The foil trim can also make a huge difference. Ensure that you have the correct amount of foil to stop the boat sliding sideways, but not too much so that the boat trips over it when it turns. The rake of the foil should result in a 'light' tiller making it easy for the helm to point the boat where they want to go.

It is a question of feel: you know, if you really focus, when it feels correct and when it doesn't. Keep a careful note of your fastest settings and the conditions they worked in, so that you can repeat them.

To achieve the same sail shape (for example leech twist) you may require far more kicker tension in 15 knots than 5 knots. 15 knots is 3 times 5 knots, but the pressure in the sail is more than 9 times greater because pressure is proportional to wind speed squared. ($15 \times 15 = 225$, $5 \times 5 = 25$.) This is why it is key to 'get your head out of the boat' to look for differences in wind speed. This can make a massive difference to your boatspeed, especially if you have optimised your rig set up.

Another fact to consider is that the waves will rarely be lined up with the wind, so one tack may be better than the other for surfing the waves. You need to get a rig set up which allows the boat to head up and bear away through the appropriate angle. For example, on one tack you may be wanting to head up more than the other. The more kicker that you have the easier it is to head up, but the harder it is to bear away and vice versa.

The key is to maximise your time going down the waves and avoid running into any hills; after all jogging downhill takes much less effort than jogging uphill. Don't look only at the wave in front of you, but the wave in front of that and the wave in front of that – this way you can choose the best route and plan where you want to go next (or when you want to gybe).

As you steer for the waves, you need to ensure that the sails are still correctly trimmed at all times: telltales can give you the information that you need, telling you whether a sail is correctly

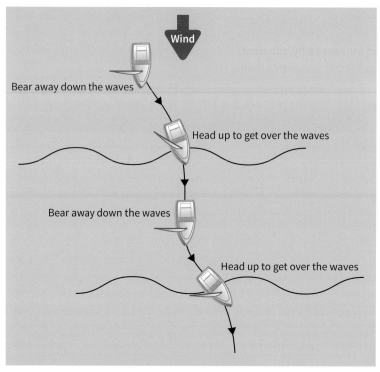

Heading up and bearing away from the waves

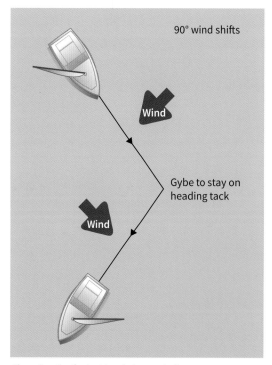

Choosing the fastest track downwind

trimmed. They should be streaming from the luff to the leech and horizontal. If they are pointing down then you need to release the sheet or kicker tension (the sail is too far in or the leech is too closed). If they are pointing up, the opposite is true. Where you position the telltales can come down to a matter of personal taste, but around six mast diameters from the luff of the sail is usually a good starting point.

Downwind you are always looking for the heading tack – the tack which takes you closest to the leeward mark or gate (just as upwind you are looking for the lifting tack to take you to the windward mark by the shortest possible route). Therefore you need to gybe on the shifts and stay in phase with the wind. So, for example, if you approach the windward mark on a starboard lift, you know there is a port header, so you want to get onto port downwind as soon as possible.

Sailing by the Lee

In unstayed boats like the Laser and Radial, sailing by the lee can be extremely fast. Here the flow of the wind goes from the leech of the sail to the luff (exiting by the mast) and you can see this from the telltales. Now the mast acts as the leech, which is very stiff and therefore very stable. Remember everything is now in reverse, so when you get a gust you want to stay in it as long as possible so you head up (rather than bear away).

One of the advantages of sailing by the lee is that you may not need to gybe, so you can stay on starboard tack for the whole run, but the main reason is for boatspeed (and it is not uncommon to see Lasers gybe several times during the run to stay mainly sailing by the lee – just like spinnaker boats gybe to stay on the headed tack).

By sailing by the lee then broad reaching you change the angle the boat is sailing by a huge amount. This can be very useful for catching waves or getting into pressure coming down one side of the run quickly. It also means that you need to move large amounts of sheet (use as thin a sheet as possible so that you can feel any changes of pressure in light wind) and body movement (to leeward to start the head up / to windward to start the bear away) to turn the boat using minimum rudder. The boats look very dynamic rolling and turning downwind to make the best use of the waves. Rather like an escalator to the downwind mark, you want to catch each and every wave – if you miss one you take a step back on the escalator.

The fastest way to go downwind is very rarely a dead run, even in a single-hander with an unstayed rig where the boom can be let out all the way to 90 degrees (without being stopped by a shroud). This is for two reasons: because you need flow over the sail either from luff to leech or (sailing by the lee) leech to luff, plus you need to find the route of least resistance through the waves, and this is very rarely going straight into them (going dead downwind is only likely to be the best course in very flat water when trying to stay in a gust for as long as possible). You only need to change the angle of the boat slightly to achieve good flow or create a better angle of attack for the waves.

In fact the death roll is caused by trying to sail the boat straight downwind with the wind constantly changing the direction of flow (from luff to leech then leech to luff). Sailors usually try to correct this with their body weight but sometimes this is not enough. The simple answer is to sheet in slightly and bear away, so that you are safely by the lee.

This is very different from the windward capsize, which is simply when the sail is too far out and pushing the boat to windward, making it capsize to windward (much as if you oversheet, the boat will be pushed to leeward and will try to capsize to leeward).

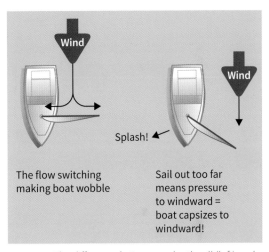

The flow switching making boat wobble

Sail out too far means pressure to windward = boat capsizes to windward!

The difference between a death roll (left) and a windward capsize (right)

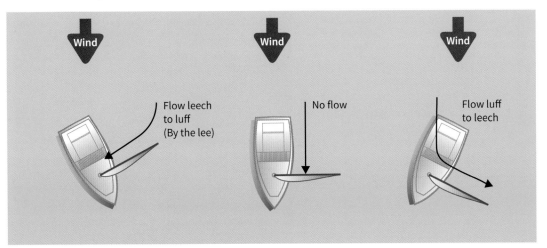

Flow leech to luff (By the lee)

No flow

Flow luff to leech

Flow of wind over the sail

If you follow one of the top Laser sailors downwind in a RIB you will see them zigzagging all over the place but overall they are sailing pretty much a straight line to the next mark (although, of course, they need to keep their wind clean from the boats behind). You would see this if you looked from a long way above, such as in a helicopter.

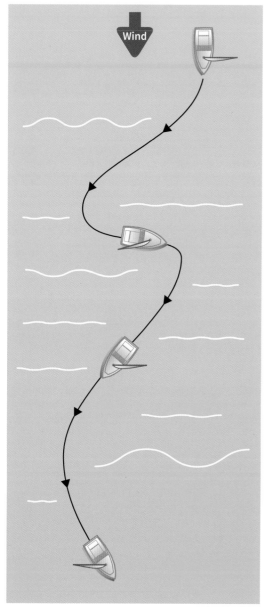

Boat sailing the best route downwind through the waves

Apparent Wind Sailing

More and more boats are influenced by apparent wind. As modern boats get faster and faster they get large amounts of apparent wind, so much so that the fastest boats in the world almost always seem to be sailing upwind!

The more the wind comes from the front, the more you need to sheet in and bear away to hold your course. This is obviously a good thing as it takes you closer to the leeward mark. So it often pays to get the boat going fast first, so that you get the apparent wind, then you can bear away – keeping your top speed and going nice and low.

The windier it is, and the faster the boat, the more apparent wind comes into play.

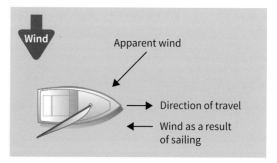

Apparent wind

It may seem strange that the first thing you need to do is to head up, to get the boat going fast, before you bear away with the apparent wind. Remember that if you are trapezing going into a gybe then there should be enough wind to trapeze going out, and you need to push the boat up to speed as quickly as possible. If the boat slows then you lose the apparent wind and you need to adjust the sails accordingly. So it is key to keep the boat going as fast as possible at all times.

Slower boats tend to sail by the true wind and faster boats, especially those with asymmetric spinnakers, will sail by apparent wind most, if not all, of the time (often there is a minimum wind speed to start races). So changing classes can be a real education, but the trend definitely seems for boats to be getting faster and more exciting, which can only be a good thing.

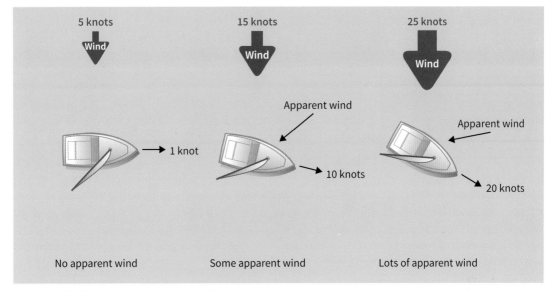

Apparent wind increases as the wind speed increases

Advice from Olympic Gold Medallist (Laser class) Paul Goodison

" The most important thing for downwind boatspeed is pressure: the more wind we have and the longer we can stay in it, the faster the boat will go. To spend the most time in the pressure it is important to sail in the direction that the pressure is travelling and then link up the next area of pressure without spending too much time in the lighter spot.

Waves are also critical to increase boatspeed. Try to keep the boat travelling down the front of waves as much as possible, and spend as little time as possible travelling up the back of them.

In Laser sailing it is also important to use the heel of the boat to assist steering, as using too much rudder will slow the boat down. Make sure the boat is heeled to windward on the bear away and heeled to leeward on the luff ups. "

CHAPTER 7

Strategy

Strategy is the way you would choose to sail around a course as quickly as possible if there were no other boats present (always with a clear wind, never having to keep clear of anyone, etc.) – just like doing a 'time trial'. Good race strategy is the way you would sail when leading a handicap race where you were the fastest boat, as opposed to sailing in a tight one-design class where you were just in the lead. Having said this, you often need another boat out there to test your strategy against: for example before the race boat A goes left, boat B goes right and they meet at the top and decide which side of the course was favoured and why.

At some venues the race strategy may be very obvious: for example, if there is a large island affecting the wind, very high land on one side of the race course or strong currents. The strategy may, of course, change over the course of the day, for example if the wind increases or the current decreases or vice versa.

Remember it is very hard to determine strategy effectively with lots of boats around, or on a short course, as often tactics will be more important here.

Strategy varies a lot from class to class and also across the wind range. In marginal planing conditions, for example, finding areas of strong wind may be the priority, whereas on a shifty day, being on the correct tack (both up and downwind) for the wind direction is crucial. The effect of current is also relative to the speed of the boat. The slower the boat the greater the effect current has.

It is a very good habit to launch early and get familiar with the conditions of the day, even if you know the venue very well. This is one of the most beautiful aspects of sailing: every day is different. However, you should look at the tidal charts for an area before you launch, as you need to consider safety: you don't want to find out the hard way!

Usually the best approach is to decide the key strategy for the day: whether that is to get into pressure, to get out of the strong adverse current or simply always to be tacking on the shifts. Sailing is a very dynamic sport: there are many variables, so you have to pay attention to the most important ones first... it probably really doesn't matter if you are being given dirty air if you are on a huge lift which is already taking you above the layline to the mark.

The key to good decision making is to have as much information as possible: both that which can be obtained beforehand through weather forecasts, studying the venue's topography and looking at tidal charts; and the information you can see by 'getting your head out of the boat', like a large black cloud coming down the course, the formation of 'sea breeze clouds' or simply by noting which side of the course seems to be paying.

You can also use the information that you have gathered early in the race to help you in the later stages, so, if the current made a big impact on the beat (either helping or hindering), then it is likely to make a big impact on the downwind legs too. This is WHY it is always so important to ask yourself WHY one side is gaining!

Ease of boat handling is also a factor as slow boats which tack fast are likely to tack much more frequently (on smaller shifts and pressure differences) than fast boats which lose a lot of ground when they tack.

The use of a dartboard can ensure that you make good strategic decisions, highlighting which elements you should concentrate on.

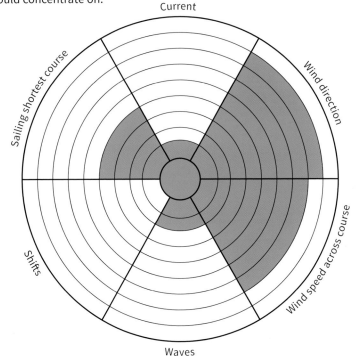

Strategic considerations dartboard

Upwind Strategy

Current

If the current is flowing in more or less the opposite direction to the wind, it obviously pays to sail towards the area of maximum flow when beating, although you need to be careful not to overstand the layline (as it will be narrower than normal). You will also have to be careful not to get OCS at the start.

If the current is flowing in the same direction as the wind, the opposite is true. You want to stay out of the strong current for as long as possible.

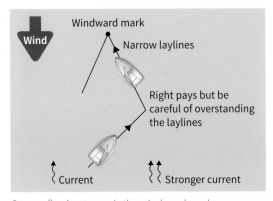

Current flowing towards the windward mark

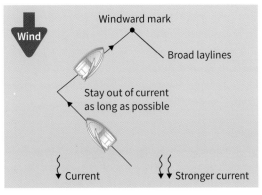

Current flowing towards the leeward mark

If the current is going across the course then there should be no difference. However if this makes the course "skewed" (you spend much more time on one tack than another) then you always want to do the long tack first to keep your options open.

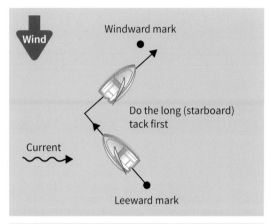

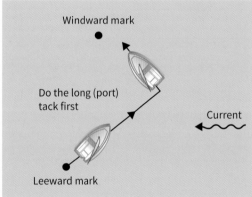

Current flowing across the course

Remember: current flows can change considerably throughout the day, so what was a good strategy in the morning may be a very bad strategy in the afternoon just because of a slight change of current. You can obtain this data from charts but it is always worth dropping a bottle of water near a mark to check this for yourself.

Wind

In the complete absence of current (sailing inland), or perhaps just if the current is very weak, the main consideration is the wind: looking at taking advantage of as many windshifts as possible –

tacking on headers upwind and gybing on lifters downwind. Although you tend to get more shifts upwind because you are sailing towards the wind, and also because you are going slower, staying on the favoured (in this case lifting) tack is very important. You would also expect more shifts with an offshore wind than an onshore one.

Obviously the reason we choose to be on the lifting tack is because it takes you closest to the windward mark and thus allows you to sail the shortest distance (and get there quicker). However the more distance you lose tacking the greater the shift needs to be before you consider taking advantage of it.

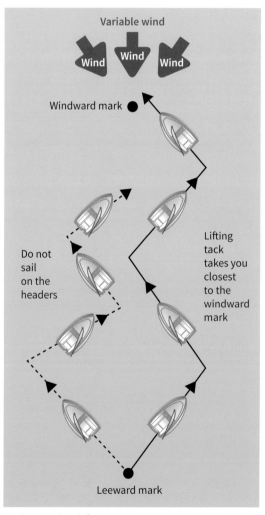

Tacking on the shifts

48

It is also worth noting that, if in doubt, when it is very shifty, always sail back towards the centre of the course, so as to keep your options open. Once you are on the layline you will only lose when the wind changes, as you will have either overstood the layline or you will have to do another two tacks and sail extra distance to pass the mark. So whenever you are in the mean wind (neither lifted or headed on either tack) sail on the tack which takes you back to the centre of the course.

By not sailing on the mean wind back to the centre of the course you have to sail on a header at the top of the beat

Windward mark

Mean wind

Lift

Header

Mean wind

Mean wind

Lift

Lift

Mean wind

Mean wind

Lift

Lift

Mean wind

Lift

Leeward mark

Staying towards the centre of the course in shifty conditions

When the land is parallel to the race course and on the left, as the wind backs over the land (in the Northern hemisphere – it is the opposite in the Southern hemisphere) there will be an area of convergence near the shore. This means that there will be more wind on the left.

If there is a headland, the wind tends to funnel around this, once again meaning that there will be more wind near the end of the headland. More wind can make a real difference to upwind boat speed.

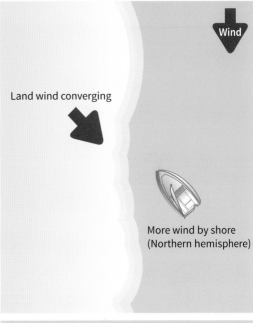

Wind

Land wind converging

More wind by shore (Northern hemisphere)

Wind converging around headland

More wind on left

Convergence means more wind

The land can have a huge effect on the wind and sometimes it is only obvious when you consider the big picture (an effect which is not obvious in a 100 metre beat may be very obvious in a 1000 metre beat). One such example of this is a wind bend caused by the land: you need to be certain that you are all the way into the wind bend before tacking or else you will sail extra distance (you need to tack at the point you get maximum lift).

change of breeze by looking at smoke coming off the land, flags on shore or other boats upwind. Here, you want to get yourself to the required side before the shift occurs, so as to be able to take full advantage of it (but once again remembering laylines).

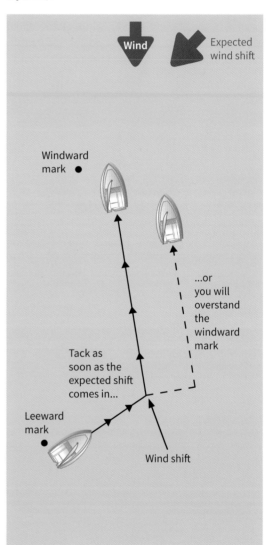

Sail towards the centre of a wind bend before tacking

Tack immediately on an expected wind shift

Sometimes you may have a persistent shift. This is one you expect, for example because of the formation of a sea breeze (watch the clouds), or perhaps the weather forecast has predicted a change of wind direction. Often you can spot the

If you know a venue very well you may be able to predict the timings of an expected shift – for example when you see all the signs of a sea breeze. In this situation it would pay to go right all afternoon.

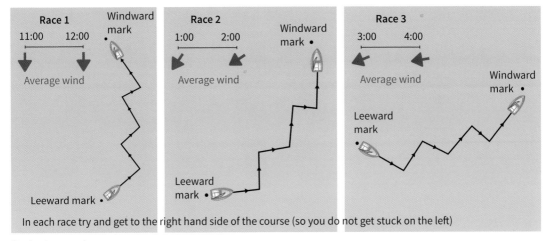

In each race try and get to the right hand side of the course (so you do not get stuck on the left)

Racing in a sea breeze

Waves

Waves are yet another factor to consider as part of your race strategy as they can have a large effect on boatspeed (both positive and negative): if you are going over the waves (sailing upwind or going downwind so fast that you can pass the wave) you want flat water; if the waves are helping you (you are surfing them), then you want big waves! You will also need to choose carefully your place to tack and gybe, to maximise the gain made towards the next mark of the course.

than following your strategy 100% (unless you are absolutely 100% sure). An all or nothing approach may win a club race or perhaps an open meeting, but will rarely, if ever, win a championship. Sailing is a sport where the race is not over until it is over; it is a consistency sport. Until you cross the finish line you are never sure of your position (and even then it can change as a result of protest!). Watch the fleet and remember that you get exactly the same number of points whether you win a race by a metre or a kilometre!

Looking to avoid the waves upwind

Consistency

A consistent approach tends to win regattas, so often playing the percentages is the best bet rather

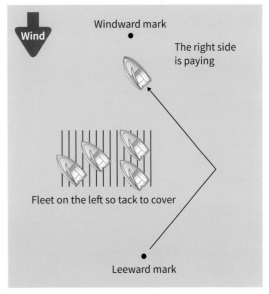

Playing the percentages

51

Downwind Strategy

Current

On a reach, the aim is usually just to minimise the distance sailed, and you can use the current to help you do this: the quickest route on a reach is a straight line (as it is the shortest distance), so the course sailed should reflect the current flow. This assumes that the wind strength remains constant, and that by going high or low you would not find an area of more wind.

Things on the run are slightly more complicated as the fleet can have quite big separations from left to right, but all sail a very similar distance to the leeward mark. On the run it will also pay to be towards the side of maximum favourable flow, and sometimes it may even pay to sail some extra distance to get into even stronger flow, or sometimes you are just using the current to minimise the distance sailed (so your actual course is dead downwind).

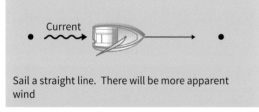

Sail towards the current. Be careful not to get pushed high / low

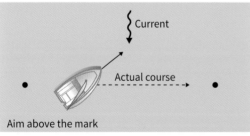

Sail a straight line. There will be more apparent wind

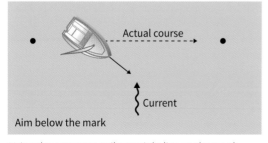

Aim above the mark

Aim below the mark

Using the current to sail a straight line on the reach

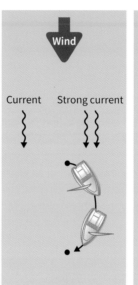

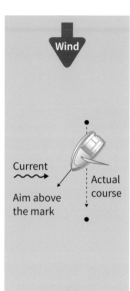

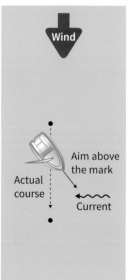

Using the current on the run

Wind

Downwind you need to gybe to sail on the headers (the favoured tack), just as upwind you tack to sail on the lifts (the favoured tack). Therefore you gybe on the lifts downwind, just as you tack on the headers upwind. This means that you sail the shortest distance to the next mark. However, in boats with unstayed rigs you may choose to sail by the lee. In this case, you will be sailing on the opposite tack, with the airflow going the other way across the sail (from leech to luff). This is often very fast and very stable. A good example of a class which does this is the Laser.

Downwind, pressure is very important, as difference in wind speed can make far more difference to boatspeed compared to upwind. Always try to position yourself so that you are lined up for the wind. The faster the boat, the more the wind approaches from the side. For example, in an Optimist, the wind will be directly from behind while, for a Nacra 17 travelling at speed, the wind will be coming much more from the side. You need to stay in the pressure for as long as possible, but take the opportunity to move back towards the centre of the course (unless all the boats are on the same side as you) to put the gains made in the bank.

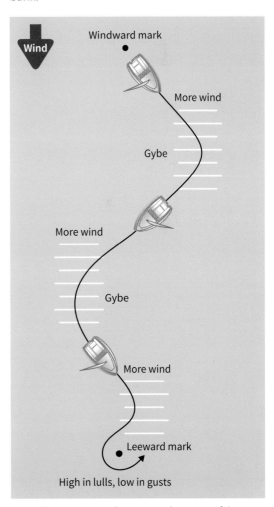

Gybing for the wind shifts (sailing broad reaching or by the lee)

Using the pressure and staying to the centre of the course

Remember: if the land is parallel to the race course, then there will be more wind on one side of the race course due to convergence / divergence. When looking upwind (in the Northern hemisphere), if the land is on the right, then there will be more wind on the offshore side of the race course; if the land is on your left then there will be more wind on the inshore side of the race course.

Pressure tends to come down the course in patches. By bearing away in the gusts it is possible to stay in them for longer, and this also enables you to head up in the lulls to maintain your average boatspeed. When sailing downwind you steer less, so pressure is king. You may need to gybe to stay in pressure. When you get the opportunity, move to sail a conservative race, but remember that an extra knot or two of breeze can make a real difference. If the wind is directly offshore, the further away from land you are (especially high land) the more pressure there will be.

If the local topography means that one side of the course has more pressure than the other, this side is then favoured both up and downwind. A good example of this would be Lake Garda.

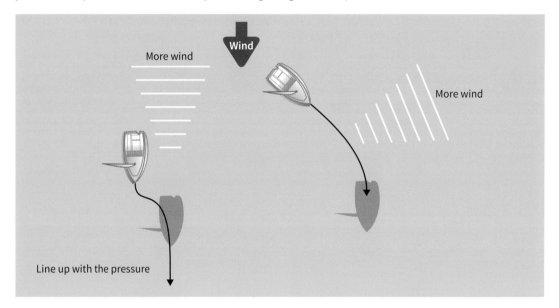

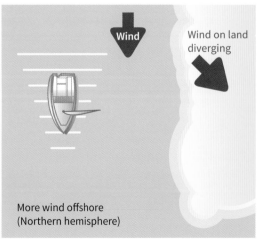

Pressure differences across the course

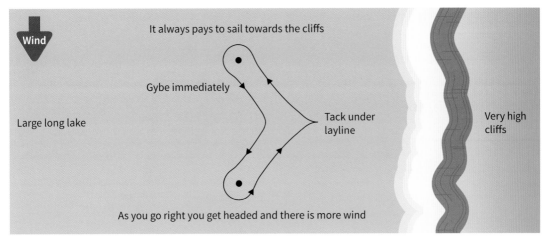

Wind

It always pays to sail towards the cliffs

Gybe immediately

Large long lake

Tack under
layline

Very high
cliffs

As you go right you get headed and there is more wind

Head for the cliffs at Lake Garda (but you still do need to pay attention to the big shifts!)

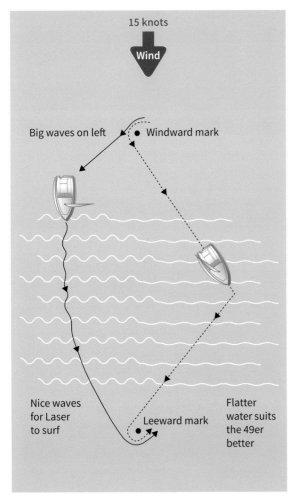

15 knots

Wind

Big waves on left   • Windward mark

Nice waves
for Laser
to surf

Leeward mark

Flatter
water suits
the 49er
better

Choosing the side of the course for the waves

Waves

Just as with sailing upwind, waves can make a real difference downwind. If you are surfing, you want to find the best ride, and this means the biggest waves (both in terms of height and length) you can catch! Whereas in light winds you do not want the waves to slow you down. In strong winds, when you can just go over them, you are looking for short wave height. This, of course, varies from boat to boat, as some boats are able to overtake the waves sooner than others.

Playing it Safe

Sailing is a complex sport and often there will be a conflict of interest: do you bear away in the gust, or do you continue to sail high, so as to get out of the adverse current quicker? Do you catch every wave, or is it best to work hard to one side of the race course? Do you need to keep away from other boats so you can sail your own race?

Wow! What a lot of questions… and you usually only know the correct answers after the race, and perhaps this is why sailing rewards those with lots of regatta experience, as they are able to recognise situations that they have been in before and react instinctively. This is why they say the more you practise the luckier you get.

Playing it safe is just as important downwind as it is upwind, and this means not going too far to one side of the course unless you are sure that there is a big advantage. You could however have a big advantage down one side of the course due to sea breeze (where there is more wind and the wind is always turning to the same direction).

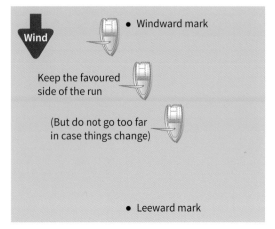

Playing it safe downwind

You need to be especially careful if the course gets skewed either due to a wind shift or due to current. Normally this will be apparent on the beat before. Maybe the mark has just drifted in the current. These things do happen, so remember to keep your head out of the boat at all times!

One of the reasons that the leader often ends up so far ahead is that they are able to sail a straight line (minimise distance) to the next mark of the

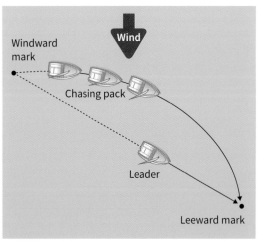

Sailing the shortest course downwind

course, whereas the boats behind are all fighting to sail over the top of each other and therefore sail a classic 'banana shape'! When you are sailing this is not so noticeable, but if there were a helicopter filming from overhead you would probably be surprised to see the result and this is why having a transit – to know you are sailing in a straight line (especially if there is strong current) – can be so useful.

Advice from Double Olympic Medallist (49er class) Simon Hiscocks

" *Strategy is all about having a plan for how, given the opportunity, you would like to sail a race: which side of the race course you would like to go to or to protect.*

A lot of strategy can be done before going on the water. Local topography will affect the wind and tides and can be checked out with a chart and tide table. There may even be a fair amount of public information regarding racing on the course areas at popular venues. Asking people who have raced at the venue beforehand, or locals, might reveal a lot of local knowledge, which, combined with the rules on wind bends, convergence and divergence, will cover most of the course scenarios.

Once on the water, try to work out what type of day it is. Is it gusty or steady? How large are the wind shifts and how fast are they? All of these factors affect a number of rules that you might create for the day, or for a particular race. Be careful of making too many rules, or at least be open minded about the rules – so that they can be changed if they don't appear to be working!

Adding this information to some of the defined factors, such as start line or course bias and any venue knowledge, will help to form a plan. It doesn't have to be a very defined plan; it can be pretty broad. For instance, it might be to start mid-line and go with the shift at the time, simply because you cannot create anything more substantial. You now know where you want to start and you know what information you are looking for. Once started there are only two options to take. It defines how the team will work and how the tactical decisions will be made. "

CHAPTER 8

Tactics

Boat-to-boat tactics are the way you race the boat considering the boats around you, in other words: how you can achieve the best overall position in a regatta. So this may mean that it is better to take a safe option and go the same side of the course as your main rivals, or even try to sail a rival down the fleet rather than try to win the race.

Match racing and team racing are the areas of the sport where tactics are most important, as boats or teams of boats are pitted directly against each other. Match and team racing are therefore an excellent way of improving tactics, as well as boat handling and use of the rules.

In the context of fleet racing, the best way to improve your tactics is short course racing: the more boats, and the greater similarity in their ability, the harder – and therefore the better – this becomes. If you can get a group together to train over a small course you can get many more races completed in a day than you usually would in a whole championship or two months of club racing!

Remember good boat handling skills are essential (as well as knowledge of the Racing Rules) before you do short course racing, as you will probably make yourself very unpopular if you keep crashing into people, especially if you are completely in the wrong. So ensure your boat handling is up to scratch (see Chapter 2).

In some races it may be necessary to beat a particular boat, perhaps to ensure qualification for a final series or to guarantee an overall result on the final day of the regatta. Here boat-to-boat tactics are vital, especially if the course is short, and this may even affect the way you tune your boat (so as to make boat handling easier).

A good example was in the 49er class where two boats, A and B, did two training sessions on the same day, in the same wind strength, with neither boat altering their rig over lunchtime. In the morning boat A won every single boatspeed test. The tuning runs were long, and over time boat A always crept ahead. However in the afternoon, doing short course racing, boat B won nearly every race as they could accelerate off the start line quicker and tack and gybe more easily to stay in phase with the shifts and pressure. This is a great example of how at any point of the race you should have a mental dartboard of your priority (in the above example: either speed or boat handling).

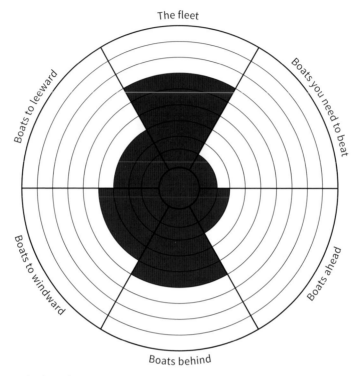

The fleet

Boats to leeward

Boats you need to beat

Boats to windward

Boats ahead

Boats behind

Tactical considerations dartboard

Upwind Tactics

Covering

The most basic upwind tactic is to cover the opposition, and this is probably the first one we learn. It works best when the fleet is well spread out and other boats are unlikely to interfere. Remember it is very hard for one boat to cover the whole fleet! So regattas are often won by the ability to sail well consistently. You cannot 'beat' every boat, although you may have to beat specific boats later in the competition. Bearing this in mind, covering is more likely to be a good tactic on the last beat than the first, unless there is an overwhelming reason to cover a specific boat.

Cover may broadly be described in two types – loose and tight (although of course it is not black and white... there are many shades of grey):

1. Loose Cover

Loose cover is when the aim is simply to stay in

front of another boat without interfering with it too much. You don't want to slow it down, but you want to make it very hard for the opposition to overtake you by staying roughly between the rival boat and the windward mark. By not giving it too much dirty wind the sailor is likely to carry on sailing. Where possible you want to avoid a tacking duel which would slow you both down.

To slow other boats down you need to give them as much dirty air as possible: this means giving them tight cover and tacking every time they do. If you are confident in your boat handling, keep as close as you dare. Each and every tack they do will lose them some ground. It rarely pays to slow someone down at the beginning of a race or series, but it may be a useful tactic at the end.

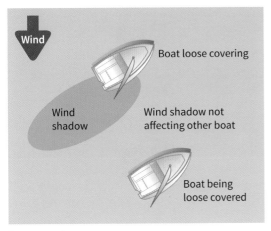

Loose covering

2. Tight Cover

Tight cover is used when the objective is to slow the other boat down or even to push it to the back of the fleet. Here you want to give it as much dirty air as possible and, as long as you are confident that your boat handling is as good as or better than the other sailor, then you welcome a tacking duel.

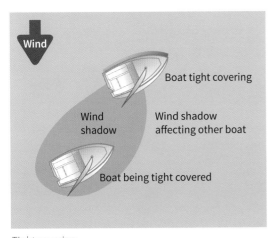

Tight covering

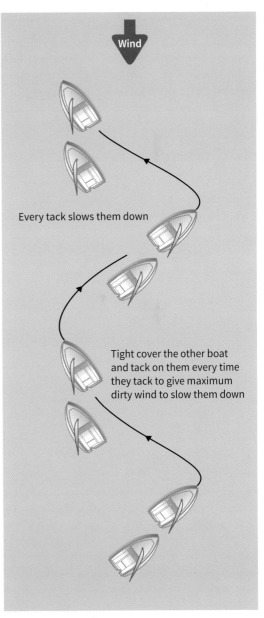

Slowing someone down

Exercise 1: Attacker & Defender

A great game to practise making and breaking cover is 'Attacker and Defender'. Here the aim is for the boat behind to overtake the boat ahead, whilst the aim of the boat ahead is to either slow down or pull away from the boat behind (remember to decide your objectives before you start the exercise).

This exercise can be done both up and downwind and the boat which is 'behind' is always considered the attacker, as it is this boat which dictates what the other boat must do to keep covering (head up, bear away, tack, gybe, etc.). Of course this exercise works best when both boats are of similar speed (choose an opponent of similar ability). It goes without saying that close observance of the rules is a must.

Upwind, the upwind boat is the defender

Downwind, the downwind boat is the defender

Attacker and defender

Controlling the Fleet

These two types of cover can also help you to control the fleet in a variety of ways.

Leading the fleet is a key skill: knowing how to encourage the fleet to follow, when to take the opportunity to pull away and when to play it safe and loose cover the boats most likely to threaten your position. By being nice to the boats behind they are likely to follow you (whereas if you sail really high or are looking as if you may roll them, they are likely to tack away).

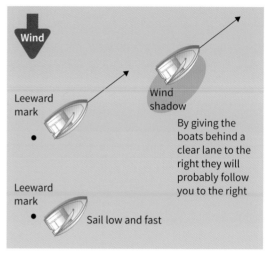

By giving the boats behind a clear lane to the right they will probably follow you to the right

Getting the fleet to follow you, in this case right

Good use of cover can help to steer your rivals where you want them to go (giving loose cover) and keep them away from where you don't want them to go (tight cover): you could do this either to force them down the fleet or to try to stop too much place changing behind you (if the whole fleet goes the same way it is very unlikely that you will get overtaken if you have good boatspeed).

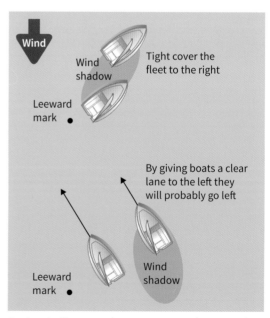

Tight cover the fleet to the right

By giving boats a clear lane to the left they will probably go left

Getting the fleet to go the way you want them to, in this case left

Sail your Own Race

However, most of the time you are not trying to slow a boat down but simply to put together a consistent series. If you can, try to work more towards the side of the course that you believe is favoured, but stay between the majority fleet and the next mark of the course. If possible, try not to hit the laylines too early (as this will limit your options).

Just remember that you still need to think of avoiding the congestion box at the windward mark (but only approach on port if you are confident of crossing the starboard boat tacks easily) and also think about the laylines and further ahead than that: the next leg of the race... are you going high or low?

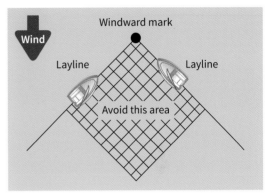

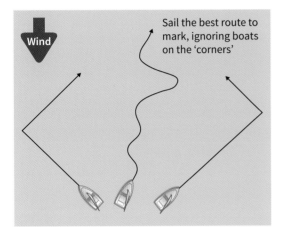

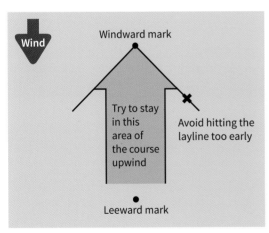

Sailing consistently

And in some conditions you may just have to sail your own race, especially if the fleet is well separated, the conditions are very shifty or there are big pressure differences. You can hardly loose cover the fleet effectively if they are in completely different wind to you, better to just get on and sail your own race.

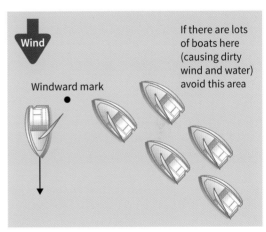

Windward mark congestion

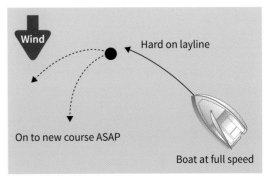

Windward mark rounding

Downwind Tactics

When going downwind, unless you have a very large lead, you are usually influenced by the boats behind you. So the key idea is usually to sail fast and this means that you need clean air. Also bear in mind that, in an effort to stay in front, a defending boat may well slow you down so, if you can keep clear of other boats, it is usually easier to maintain good boatspeed. You also need to remember this when turning to sail back upwind.

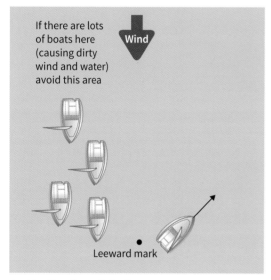

Avoid sailing through the fleet

Get your head out of the boat: tactics downwind can often be decided on the upwind leg or even on the previous downwind leg if you are in the second half of a race. You need to decide if you are sailing your own race or attacking or defending: this will depend upon the number of boats around you and their distance from you.

In a perfect world you will do as many open meetings as possible before going to National or even International events to ensure that, when you encounter a difficult situation (someone gybes on you, starts to luff, etc.), you instinctively react the right way.

Often it is a case of risk management. If the boats behind you are a long way behind, you can afford to attack those in front; if the situation were reversed then maybe you need to think more about defending your position. Of course, in the absence of boats close by, you sail your own race: just looking to get into the pressure / favoured current, etc., first.

Exercise 2: Downwind

Practice makes perfect and again short course racing is ideal for tactics, in this case downwind. Begin upwind and line up in a follow-my-leader on a beam reach then do a leeward, windward, leeward course. If you want to make the boat handling more difficult than just a bear away, do a tack, then bear away (make sure you have enough room between the boats to do this).

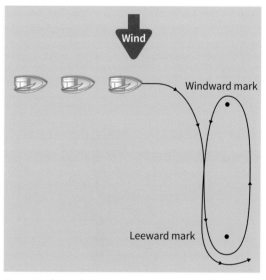

Downwind exercise

Downwind tactics start the moment you round the windward mark. You would want to put any extra distance you have in the bag and remember you will nearly always be going faster downwind than upwind, so the space can open up really quickly. So correct positioning is very important.

You have three options:
1. Overtake to windward.
2. Sail as fast as you can.
3. Overtake to leeward.

1. Overtake to Windward

Establish an overlap and overtake by covering the leeward boat until you overtake (be careful not to get into a luffing battle which slows you both down) or simply get room at a downwind mark.

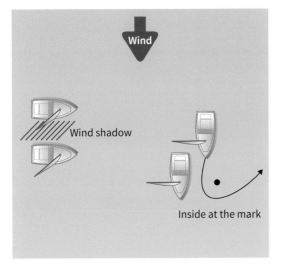

Overtaking to windward

2. Sail as Fast as you Can

Simply point at the next mark of the course. If you are behind someone (and giving them wind shadow) they may move out of your way. On a reach encourage the boat in front to keep going rather than go high.

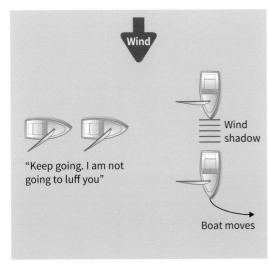

Going straight to the mark

3. Overtake to Leeward

You may do this to go under boats which are sailing too high or to get water at the leeward mark.

Remember that you need to give yourself plenty of space to leeward so that you are not in too much wind shadow.

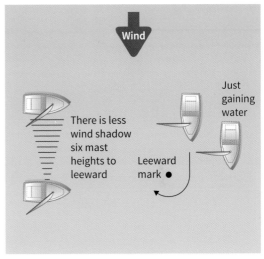

Overtaking to leeward

Defending

As a defending boat, often your best defence is simply to sail fast. If you have to be aggressive, one short sharp luff is probably better, rather than a long slow one, where you both sail lots of extra distance. Be clear that you will not tolerate being overtaken just to windward (but if a boat goes really high, so that they will not give you dirty air... let them go!).

Leeward Mark Rounding

Remember that the best opportunity to overtake is often at marks. It can be worth slowing down to avoid doing a bad leeward mark rounding or to capitalise on someone else's, as clean air up the beat is very important.

A good leeward mark rounding is also essential so that you have clean wind for the upwind leg. You can easily undo all of your hard work downwind with a sloppy leeward mark rounding and make life very difficult for yourself up the next beat.

You need to get as many of the sail controls

sorted before rounding the mark and give yourself a wide enough entrance to the mark to ensure a tight exit. In a perfect world, if a picture were taken just one boat length after the mark, you should not be able to tell that you have just rounded it. So whenever training always finish on a good leeward mark rounding, as it is such an important skill.

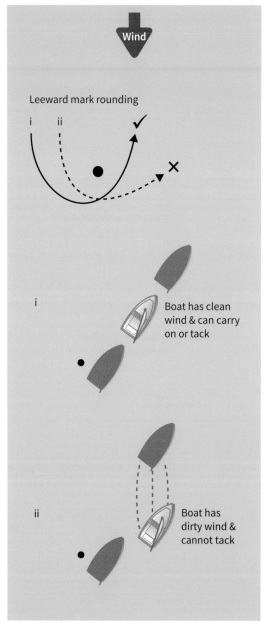

A good leeward mark rounding

Summary of Key Ideas

* Keep your wind clear or get into clean wind as soon as possible.
* Stay between the opposition and the next mark (directly upwind on the upwind legs, slightly offset on the downwind legs so as to have clean wind).
* Protect the favoured side of the course (the side with more wind, better current, etc.).

Advice from Olympic Gold Medallist (Laser class) Paul Goodison

" *I feel the key to tactics is being able to adapt quickly to changing situations. It is very much about weighing up the risk / reward for each action on the race course. Try to minimise risk and sail conservatively. Generally, the people who make the fewest mistakes win.*

It is important to be able to focus on the right thing at the right time. Different weather conditions and fleet positions will require different tactics. I try to keep things as simple as possible, and set myself small goals for different conditions. For example, in shifty conditions, I will always be on the lifted tack, sometimes even if this means that I am in dirty air. In stable conditions, I always make sure that I have clear wind. This may mean that I have to take a small header to clear my lane. I set out these goals for each day, as they are dependent on the conditions and stage of the regatta. It is easy to overcomplicate this area of sailing: generally the people that are winning are just keeping it simple. "

CHAPTER 9

Rules

Before you start playing any game you need to know the rules: if you were playing football (soccer to American readers) then you would soon be pretty unpopular if you kept on picking up the ball with your hands and running with it. You would keep on getting sent off the pitch and pretty soon no one would want to play with you! Well this is also true in sailing.

You need to have a basic knowledge of the rules before you go on the water, just as you need to know all the moves chess pieces can make before you consider sitting down to play a game. If you don't know the rules then, at best, you may spend some serious time in the protest room and get disqualified and, at worst, someone could be seriously hurt in a nasty collision. Remember sailing is a self policing sport: if you break a rule...

do something about it.

You can download the Racing Rules for free from *www.sailing.org* but remember it is important not only to know the rules but also to be clear about the definitions.

The most important section of the rules to have a good understanding of is Part Two, which deals with when boats meet. This can simply be considered as five sections:

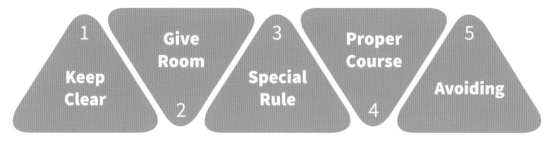

1. Keep Clear

10	Port / Starboard
11	Windward / Leeward
12	Astern / Ahead
13	Tacking
19.2 (c)	Overlap at continuing obstruction
22.1	Returning to the start
22.2	Penalties
22.3	Backwards

2. Give Room

15	Acquiring right of way

16	Right of way changing course
18	Passing marks
19	Passing obstructions
20	Room to tack

3. Special Rule

18.3	Tacking in the zone

4. Proper Course

17	Not above a proper course
18.4	Inside boat gybing at a mark

5. Avoiding

So when you get the chance read through the rules. You will be able to race with far more confidence afterwards.

As well as always having a rule book with you, I would also strongly recommend buying one of the excellent books which explain the rules. My personal favourite is Bryan Willis' book *The Rules in Practice*.

Using the Rules Aggressively

Approaching a mark is often your best opportunity to overtake another boat. So here aggressive tactics can really pay off: ensuring that you gain overlap when entering the mark room zone or, if you are the lead boat, sailing in such a way to break the overlap 'at the very last minute' – in both situations this is achieved by crucially altering the angle of your boat.

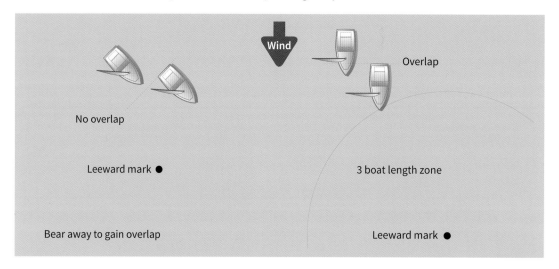

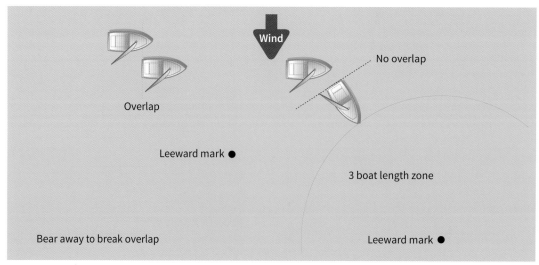

Room at the mark

This tactic of altering the angle of the boat also works at the finish where at the very last minute you want to sail perpendicular to the finish line to finish as soon as possible (which may mean going near head to wind or straight downwind).

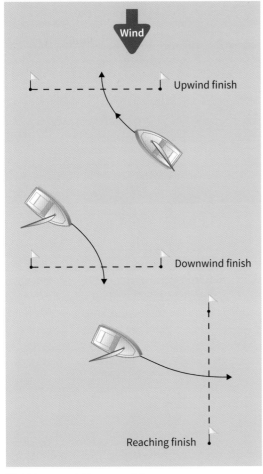

Finishing as quickly as possible

Of course another area where boats always come together is at the start. Here having space to leeward makes it much easier to have a good start, and a good start makes it much easier to have a good race. So you want to protect your gap to leeward whilst at the same time not giving the boat to windward too big a gap so she can easily accelerate over you. To create a bigger gap you may consider doing two quick tacks.

Remember as you approach on port you are a give way boat to a starboard boat until you complete your tack underneath (the bow must go down to a close-hauled course for the tack to be complete). Now the rules change... and it is now the windward / leeward rules that apply.

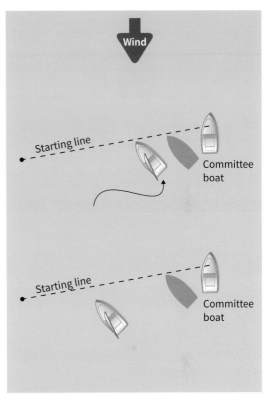

Slotting into leeward

Using the Rules Defensively

One of the biggest secrets to sailing fast is having your own space and the ability to sail your own race. This means being in clean wind, clean waves and good wind (both in terms of pressure and direction). So, as much as anything, this means trying to avoid bad situations.

The 'slam dunk' is where a boat tacks right on your wind, giving you maximum amount of dirty wind and leaving you trapped. The key to avoiding a slam dunk is to leave the bearing away to the last possible moment and then squeezing up as soon as you pass the other boat's stern (so as to close the gap she can tack into).

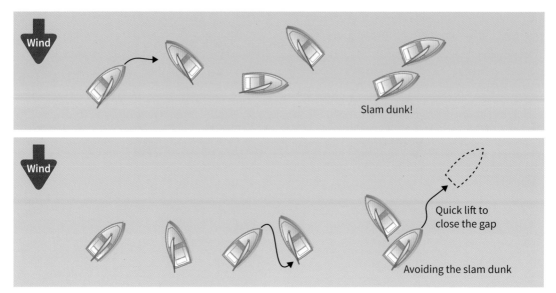

To avoid the slam dunk bear away late and luff quickly

Likewise, when approaching the windward mark you want not only to avoid boats giving you dirty wind from windward but also boats tacking close under you to leeward and slowing you down. So try to approach the windward mark slightly footing: sailing fast and free for the final few boat lengths so that if someone does tack underneath you, you can simply luff and keep your wind clean, whilst maintaining good speed.

Remember that you do not have to alter course until their tack is complete and, inside the three boat length zone, boats cannot tack if it forces you to sail above a close-hauled course. For this reason tacking inside the three boat length zone is not a good idea in a tightly packed fleet (this is not a problem if you are well clear of surrounding boats).

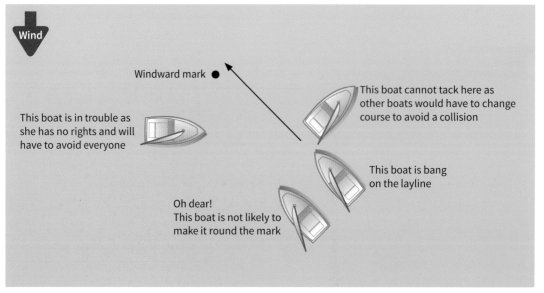

Windwark mark approach

Advice from Olympic Gold Medallist (Radial class) Lijia Xu

" As a sailor you need to know by heart the basic rules in Part Two, Section A of the Racing Rules of Sailing (RRS) to start with. Starboard / port, windward / leeward, clear ahead / clear astern are the situations we most frequently confront during a race. Its main purpose is to avoid contact in all kinds of boat-to-boat scenarios by a give way boat keeping clear of a right of way boat. Later on you start to handle more complicated rules such as rules 14 to 24 in Sections B & C. These help you to analyse the many different situations around marks / obstructions, tacking / gybing, acquiring right of way / changing or proper course / unusual manoeuvres, etc.

An effective way to learn the rules is to read the Case Book and Call Book, which are both authorised interpretations of the RRS. You can try to analyse 3-5 quizzes every evening before bed. Always re-read the Definitions and Rules that applied in each case to make sure you fully understand it. Before long you will find yourself not only mastering the rules better and

better, but you also gradually become a tactically-wise sailor which improves your overall racing level.

In the next stage you get to learn some of the procedure rules as a necessary race preparation, i.e. protest / redress, conduct of a race / other requirements. Being familiar with these rules will guide you on how to preserve your right as a participant in any regatta.

In the end, nothing can replace the real experience in a protest hearing. Whenever there is a chance to protest or request for redress in practice regattas, go for it! Those accumulated authentic experiences will no doubt help you to handle the big pressure with confidence in performance regattas.

Last but not least, be fair and honest: this is what we owe to this lifetime sport. Sailing is a self-governed sport: we want to protect the pure joy which fascinates us the most and keeps attracting more and more people around the world to join the sailors' family. "

CHAPTER 10

The Winning Mind

Races are often won and lost before you even hit the water. It is not enough just to be physically fit – your head has to be 'in the right place' to win. You not only need to be physically tough, you also need to be mentally tough, and, at the end of the day, it is often the mental rather than the physical attributes that decide who are true sailing champions.

The Winning Attitude

It is about being focused, or more specifically: a *positive* focus. Don't let anyone tell you what you cannot do. Positive thinking yields positive results, and whilst failure is a stepping stone to success, the way you handle it defines you: not only as a sailor but also as a human being. We learn more from our mistakes than we do from our successes and in order to get tougher we need to put ourselves in tough situations, which is why the leap from youth to adult or from National to International sailing can seem so big.

Even if your aspirations are simply to do well at your local club, these skills will surely help you. Think how close races are; sometimes less than a second between boats, and even at the end of many championships the points are unbelievably close. The race is never over until you have crossed the line and it is this quiet determination to do the best you can which defines the most successful people in all fields of life, not just sailing.

One of the reasons why sailing is so demanding is the amount of mental concentration that is required. You need to be focused on the right thing, at the right time, and be focused all the time. This means knowing when to switch between boatspeed and when to 'get your head out of the boat', about your tactics in relation to other boats and when to consider the big picture: the race strategy. Sometimes you need to be prepared to make a small loss for a larger gain later. So the correct attitude is one of calm determination.

The problem is that when we really want something (whether it be winning our first club race or an Olympic medal), we put pressure on ourselves, and too much pressure can have a detrimental effect on our racing. The trick is to treat each and every race the same, so it becomes a good habit. After all, you never get stressed about brushing your teeth, you hardly need to think about it! Try not to look at the results too much, just check your scores are correct. There is no need to worry about anybody else's results until near the end of an event – that is beyond your control. Focus on your own racing and try to pick up the minimum number of points each day. This means keeping your head clear and focused.

Of course some people may be too relaxed. They have got used to not winning and so don't put enough pressure on themselves. So like many things in life the answer is somewhere in the middle:

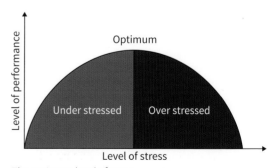

The optimum level of stress

A good routine is really helpful. Whether you need to get fired up or calm down, simply knowing exactly when you need to leave the house, when you need to leave the slipway and the order and way you are going to do everything in between can be a real help. Different routines suit different people, so you need to find out what works for you and, whether it is racing or training, you need to approach it with a professional attitude.

Sailing is a sport where it pays to be patient: there can be lots of waiting around to sail or you may have to do lots of races to complete a series. So the question is: when the going gets tough, can you keep going or do you let frustration get the better of you?

Times of stress can make things harder. You will notice that when you are tired and hungry it can have a huge effect on your mood: perhaps you become more emotional or, when under pressure, you may well get loss of appetite or stomach ache. As part of a healthy lifestyle you should always try to get adequate rest and nutrition, but especially so when you are pushing yourself hard. This applies mentally as well as physically: hydration and sun protection are especially important to help keep a clear mind, focused on the job in hand. However hard you find it, go out, do your best and remember to enjoy it!

Dealing with Disappointment

One of the most beautiful things about sailing is how each and every race is so different. Even at the most 'reliable' venues in the world things can change. When we look at a sailing series, the final result is often decided by the worst result you have to count in the series, not by how many good results you have. It is how you handle the poor start, perhaps the race after an OCS, which can determine how the event goes overall.

There are so many variables in sailing and nearly all of them are beyond our control, but those same variables (wind, waves, current, etc.) are beyond the control of all the other sailors too. It is how to handle these variables which is important. Remember that huge shift that went

against you… well it might go *for* you later in the race. Just keep sailing as fast as you can.

When something bad happens it is very easy just to focus on it. After all, if you remember it in detail, you will probably have a good story for the bar afterwards or even your blog… but is this going to help your race? NO! You need to get on with the race (and you can worry about what happened on shore, and maybe think how to prevent it from happening again, but during the race you need to be racing). Find something good to focus on. Maybe on a windy day just work really hard to keep the boat flat; on a light wind day 'get your head out of the boat' and see where the new pressure is coming from. If you are fully focused on the helpful things, it can be hard to focus on things which are unhelpful and you can help other crew members to do the same.

The exact method of refocusing, of course, depends upon the individual, and as you get more experience you get to know yourself better. Perhaps, if you have a series of disappointments, you need to take some time out, away from the sport. Motivation is a key part of a winning attitude, as everything in life worth having is achieved through hard work and hard work requires motivation. Sometimes, if you take a step back, it is easier to see the bigger picture and what issues really need to be resolved.

Relaxing

In order to be focused you also need to be able to relax. It may sound like a contradiction in terms but you cannot be 'switched on' all the time. Remember that the body and the mind are very linked. Take ten deep breaths with your belly, this relaxes your body and that will, in turn, relax your mind. (If you need to get psyched up the opposite is true: you need to get the heart rate going!)

Key words can really help here. They can anchor you to a moment in the past where you felt calm and confident. A simple reminder like "flat is fast". Just remember in detail how the tiller felt, what the boat sounded like, how heavy the sheet felt in your hand and how the sails looked. If you have done it before then you can do it again. Just like the snooker player potting the black for the 10,000th time.

Maybe a key phrase is useful. We call this positive affirmation. "I am always fast in strong winds" or "These are my favourite conditions". A positive phrase can be especially useful to break some negative thinking. You may even want to distract yourself physically. Just quietly pat yourself a couple of times and tell yourself you can do it (or better get a team mate to do it for you).

Remember the first time you do something it can be difficult (your first race win, first regatta win, first championship win, etc.) but, like everything in life, it gets easier the more you do something. Whatever happens, banish the excuses and give it 100%. No one can ask for more than that.

Advice from Olympic Gold Medallist (Radial class) Lijia Xu

"" *The heat was on in the last day of the London Olympic Games back on 6th August 2012, with four countries sharing the same chance to become the Olympic Champion in the Laser Radial medal race. Thanks to all the mental preparation I had done over the years, I was able to perform at my best under great pressure.*

Actually when I went back to campaign for London in April 2011 I had only one year and three months to prepare. But when I combined psychological exercises with everyday training, my progress soared with ultra-effective training. I would meditate before each sailing session, picturing the ideal movements and skills I wanted to achieve. I created a positive self-talk list to remind myself at each session on the water. I wrote many positive affirmations to cultivate new habits or beliefs, which were usually stuck on walls, obvious enough for me to read several times a day.

While on the race course, sailors have to be their own coach to have a clear mind guiding themselves what to do, where to focus, etc. We cannot easily allow our emotions to engulf our wits whenever a high-pressure situation comes. Instead we ought to have a calm, firm and confident mental state to lead us to make the right calls every time. ""

Lijia Xu - Positive Affirmation (Olympic Champion)

I am the 2012 World Sailing Championship Laser Radial Class Gold Medallist, the best female athlete of Chinese sports and World Sailor of the Year. Sailing under the union flag, receiving a gold medal and hearing the national anthem being played in an incredibly proud sound is the best and most exhilarating experience in my career. I have taken my next step toward the accomplishment of my lifelong goal - becoming an Olympic champion.

I enjoy the recognition as one of the best sailors in the world. I love being on the water in all conditions and am keen to perform the best I can in my sport. When I am racing I commit my all, body and soul, and nothing else matters. I control every element I am able to and have zero tolerance to any other considerations. I get my own preparation right, leave nothing to chance and take nothing for granted. I am ultra-cautious about the rules and play it safe all the time. I keep my composure, stay quietly confident and think radically in crucial junctures. I am good at dealing with all kinds of problems and not letting it affect my performance in any way.

I am very physical and ultra-aggressive once I hit the water, but a really nice girl and revert to my normal self of daily routines while on land. I train hard in the gym and sail smart on the water. Now I am incredibly fit, highly motivated and extremely well prepared - I know clearly I am here to win. I am at my peak and my body can withstand the rigour that is to come.

All my preparation has been designed to convince my opponents that they are fighting for Silver. I always run a mental program before each racing day and reinforce each successful leg by saying: "THAT'S LIKE ME!". I record my performance analysis, and read and visualise my positive affirmation daily.

I am the National Games, World Championship, and World Cup Champion of women's Laser Radial Class sailing. Go on Lily, go for it. I know I have the edge.

Written by Lijia one year before the London 2012 Olympics, and read every day prior to The Games

CHAPTER 11

Fitness

First of all, fitness has to be fun. In the long term no one is going to do fitness training if they don't enjoy it, not unless there is a very large reward. However, there is: being fit enough to make the boat go fast is certainly much more fun than not being fit enough and being slow. After all you must be the sort of person who would like to win races to be reading this book (and to have got this far!). The trick is to get the fitness in a fun way. If a 2 hour bike ride passes in the blink of an eye in some beautiful countryside, and 20 minutes on a treadmill inside seems like hell… it is obvious which one you should be doing.

What is Fitness?

Fitness, more than ever, is a part of modern sailing, but what do we mean by 'being fit'? Quite simply it can be the difference between winning and losing, and the word 'fitness' just means being fit to do the job. It is obvious that someone who weighs 140 kgs is unlikely to be fit to be a good jockey (just think of the poor horse), whereas someone who weighs only 40 kgs won't be as suitable to lift heavy weights. The horse would run away from the 140 kg man and the 40 kg person would not try to lift the same weight as the 140 kg person! These are extreme examples but you must admit that it is pretty easy to tell the difference between an Optimist and a Finn sailor (a less extreme example).

To be clear, fitness is different from size and weight, although, of course, they can be related. You can never be too strong, too fast or too flexible, but you can be too big or too small and most classes have optimum weight ranges and suit certain sizes of people.

The key to achieving a high level of fitness is continued effort with appropriate rest and nutrition. Over training can be just as dangerous as under training and we need to be careful about our health; doing our best to avoid illness and injury.

The human body is a wonderful 'machine'. If you asked a 40 horse power engine to do the work of a 60 horse power engine it would, sooner or later, break; but with a human body it can adapt, become stronger, and sooner or later become the 60 horse power engine, and then 70, and so on. You need good sleep, good food and hard work, which may well result in large amounts of muscle soreness the next day (DOMS - Delayed Onset Muscle Soreness) but it is worth it to be the best possible you.

There are three reasons to work on your fitness:
1. To carry out successfully the job you are required to do.
2. To ensure that your body stays in balance by working on your weak areas.
3. To prevent injury.

In order to obtain the highest level of fitness, and to achieve all three of the above, it is important to look critically at all aspects that contribute to overall fitness levels, and then focus on the individual aspects that are most important for the class of boat you sail and the role that you have.

There are four key aspects that contribute to overall fitness, which can be easily remembered as *The Four Ss*:

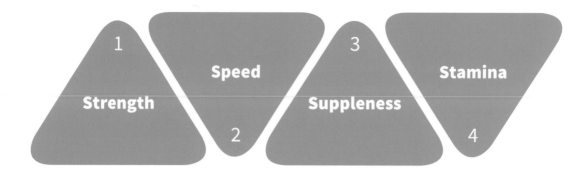

1. Strength: *The ability to lift a heavy load*

If you are not strong enough to do the job, you have to get strong enough or you could injure yourself. The best place to improve strength is in a gym – in a controlled environment with someone helping you.

A good example of a role which requires high strength is a trimmer on a keelboat – they would need to focus most on this aspect of fitness.

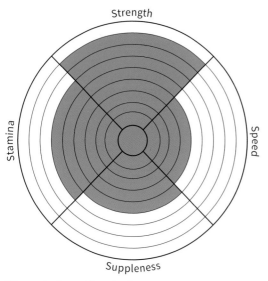

Fitness dartboard for a keelboat crew

2. Speed: *The ability to be quick (and agile) around the boat*

This is obviously a skill for the high performance skiff sailors. Maybe you don't need to be full speed all the time but, if you have the ability to move fast and accurately, it can help you out when you really need it.

3. Suppleness & Core Strength: *Being flexible but stable in the core*

Perhaps the most important, but most overlooked, part of fitness. Muscles not only need to be strong, they also need to be long, allowing you to function properly (giving full range of motion). Injuries can happen not only because muscles are not strong enough, but also if they are very tight / short (the better the flexibility, the better the chance of avoiding injury).

The 'core' muscles are especially important. Not only do they make your boat go fast, as any body movements transfer the energy to the boat better but, perhaps more importantly, they protect your lower back, and anyone who has ever suffered back pain (either because of sailing or something else) will know how painful this can be. Remember any significant damage to your back will stay with you for life, so don't take the chance... you only get one body.

4. Stamina: *The ability to keep going*

Stamina is an old fashioned word; in more modern terminology: aerobic fitness. This is determined by the power of your heart and your lung capacity.

Even on light wind days, being aerobic fit is a great benefit. People who have good aerobic fitness tend to be able to stay focused for longer, and aerobic training has also been shown to improve memory.

On the windy days (particularly in a single-hander like a Laser) it will make it easier to work hard at a high heart rate AND also help you to recover quicker for the next day's racing. Just like lifting weights you can keep a careful log of your 'heart workouts' (intensity and duration).

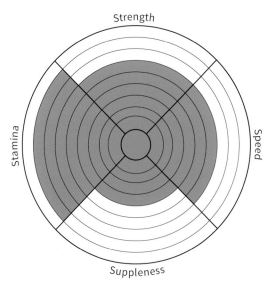

Fitness dartboard for a Laser sailor

Improving your Fitness

It is not possible to gain all of the fitness you need from your sailing. For one thing you would probably end up with some fairly serious muscle imbalances for doing just this one type of sport. For example hikers would get strong quadriceps (front / top of the thighs) and relatively weak hamstrings (back of the thighs). You also need to push your body harder than it usually is in racing to be sure that you can cope with extreme conditions or when very fatigued: pushing your core harder or your heart rate higher than you would normally do when racing.

Adaptations to your body take time, so make sure you give yourself enough time; start slowly and build up. Often you need a minimum amount of equipment (perhaps just a good pair of trainers to improve your stamina if you live in a good running area). Working hard over the winter, when there is less racing, means that you can reap the benefit in the summer months.

Proper Preparation Prevents Poor Performance. Your time is precious: make the best of it. Have a goal for each and every training session. Don't just go to the gym and 'lift a few weights'. Go to the gym and work your back / go to the gym and increase your aerobic ability / go to the gym and burn fat; go with a goal and succeed, and then afterwards eat well and get a good night's sleep. You not only need protein for muscle recovery but also carbohydrates for fuel and nutrition to keep healthy.

Each session should be like a good novel: with a beginning, a middle and an end. A warm up to prepare you for exercise is a good way to begin, the meat in the sandwich comes next and then you finish with the core and a good stretch. Never be tempted to miss the final bit when time is short (just have less meat). You need to do the core last so that it is strong to protect you when exercising, and your stretches are best done when you are really warm as they can then form a good part of your cool down routine.

Consider muscles like toffee. When they are cold they are brittle and they can easily break. When they are warmer they are much more flexible. Don't stretch when cold after sailing. If necessary do a small aerobic session when you get home. After all, this active recovery helps eliminate waste products from the muscles. Then do your stretch and maybe some self massage if areas are still sore. If you are sore, your body is trying to tell you something!

Injury prevention is part of any good training programme. Think how quickly you can lose fitness with a bad injury: it is not worth the risk. So always warm up and stretch afterwards. Keep a training diary so that you can monitor your training; ensuring that you are not over training or under training (it is amazing how those missed / extra sessions can mount up) and to see if you are resting enough (usually at least one day a week). You may find it an excellent motivational tool to look back and see all the progress you have made.

In each session, whether it is aerobic, core, strength, etc., you need to push yourself by always making the bar higher, for example:

Time

If you only ever cycle for 30 minutes, you will just get good at cycling for 30 minutes. Gradually increase the time: 30, 35, 40 minutes: you will be amazed at how quickly the time builds up, especially if you have some friends to cycle with. As a rule of thumb, you will want to do some sessions for at least 25% longer than race time (for example Laser sailors racing for 60 minutes should do longer sessions of a minimum of 75 minutes, but perhaps much, much longer than this: remember we have three or more races a day sometimes).

Type

Change the type of exercise that you are doing, even if for no other reason than to make it more interesting. You may find a 'better' exercise or perhaps just one that you enjoy more. Maybe the weather suddenly becomes nice for training outdoors: take advantage of it.

Intensity

Just like time, you can gradually increase the weight you lift or the heart rate you keep. The fitter you are the more you push yourself and the better you will get.

Frequency

Perhaps just do more of the same thing. If four sets no longer give you muscle soreness, do five or even six. Maybe as your recovery improves you can do four rather than three aerobic sessions a week.

When starting any new routine you need to be careful. You are never too young to start working the core, but for those young sailors who are still growing, when lifting heavy weights I would suggest you keep to about 70% of the maximum you can lift. It is also good to start light, so that you can get really good technique. Then this can become a lifelong habit. Nothing wrong with just starting with the bar, and practice makes perfect.

Keep working the opposite muscles too. Just as the inner tummy muscles support the lower back, the inner back muscles support the shoulders and hold them in the correct position.

Above all enjoy it. You will be able to see the results of all of your hard work both on the results sheet and in the mirror.

Looking After your Body

Advice from Olympic Gold Medallist (Radial class) Lijia Xu

> *I used to suffer numerous injuries on my knees, shoulder and lower back during my sports career. Those hindered my training and racing to such an extent that I nearly gave up sailing at some points. Past experience told me that avoiding injuries is the first priority of fitness improvement.*
>
> *So make sure you have a good foundation of a strong core – to sustain the arduous training intensity and volume – before undertaking any sports, including a serious (competitive) sailing campaign towards your long-term goal. This involves torso stability training with the aim of strengthening small muscle groups and joints around your shoulders, lower tummy and gluteus.*
>
> *At the same time it is also important to have a good posture all the time during your daily life: neck long (feeling tall by imagining a line pulling through the centre of your head), shoulders back and down, tummy in, etc. These small good habits will benefit your general health throughout your life whilst boosting your ability in sports performance. Pilates is an extremely useful exercise system to help protect the spine while maximising your flexibility, which also plays a crucial role in preventing injuries.*
>
> *Recovery is another issue that can be under-played. All too often people focus fully on strength and cardio training, but pay no attention to regeneration. The level of recovery is closely linked with the progress of fitness. Physical training is actually a muscle-damaging process; it is only those resting periods that give your body the chance to rebuild itself, making it stronger and tougher over time.*
>
> *After you realise this simple theory, I believe no one will begrudge giving their body sufficient time to recuperate. What I normally do is go for a light cardio session after strong wind sailing, whether it be jogging, running or cross-trainer, followed by a deep, relaxing full body stretch. One of my other favourite routines is doing some self-massage using a form roller, double-ball or rolling stick while reading, watching TV or before bed. All of these together cost less than*

one physio (sports) massage and are easy and light to carry as well! Why not utilize those leisure times to do some whole body massage for yourself after intensive training, to help you recover more quickly and be fresh / energetic for the next day's challenge. **99**

Lijia Xu stretching after physical training – the key to injury prevention

CHAPTER 12

Preparation & Note Taking

Proper preparation is necessary for a good performance. Lack of boat work can lead to the boat breaking which can be expensive in terms of time, money and your regatta performance, but it is more than that. Many hours can be spent on the boat productively to give you that extra edge, speed or boat handling advantage. Ensure the control systems are optimised and make every possible effort to maximise boatspeed. The minimum level necessary is to get the boat around the course with nothing breaking, but when considering a competition like the America's Cup, no expense is spared to have the lightest possible equipment, the best possible hull finish, etc., etc.

Preparing your Boat

Preparing the boat involves carefully studying the class rules and, if necessary, getting the boat measured (to show that everything complies). You need to be completely familiar with the equipment that you race with and this may change with the conditions. Perhaps you save your favourite sails and mast for the most important event of the year and train with older equipment. You need to ensure that you have significant spares and the tools required to change them: for example screw drivers, spanners, knife, lighter, fid (splicing needle) and the appropriate ropes and whipping twine.

You want:
- The lightest, stiffest and best finished hull.
- The 'best for you' spars, sails and foils (remember that different crew weights may suit different mast / foil / sail characteristics).
- Easy to operate control systems.
- Replacements for all of the above, if practical.

A good routine is to wash the boat immediately after sailing, so as to remove any salt water and mud / sand / grit from the equipment. This is also an opportunity to check the boat before putting it away.

Always do any boat work sooner rather than later as it can be easy to underestimate how long a job will take, especially if you haven't done it before. This also means that, if you need to order a part or get a specific tool for a job, you have time to do so. Remember small scratches to the hull and foils can easily be removed with sand paper: it is only a moment's work. Check any rivets for corrosion and the spars for general wear and tear... there are nearly always signs of damage before something breaks so, if in doubt, replace it.

Wear and tear can be kept to a minimum with due care and attention; keep your foils and masts in bags, sails out of the sun and just generally be careful!

When you have the time, test equipment to make sure you are 100% happy with your boat set up. It is rarely a good idea to use completely new equipment for the first time at a major championship and, if you are chartering / borrowing a boat, get out early to make sure you are happy with it.

Keeping a Racing Log

You want to be as good as you can be and this means that you should analyse your successes (so you can repeat them) and your mistakes (so you can correct them). Even after the most difficult race you should always try to debrief yourself. Look for the positives. You often learn more from your failures than your successes and, most important, record things so that there is no chance to forget. It is just a moment's work and can save you huge amounts of frustration later by helping to prevent you from making the same mistakes again.

Simply make some RAP notes (Relevant, Accurate and Precise): the wind strength and direction, the wave type, your rig set up. Remember that there can be a huge difference between 8 knots and choppy waves and 8 knots and flat water. It is the same as with the physical training, where you need to record the precise weight you lifted, the number of repetitions and the number of sets. You can then look back at this to encourage yourself with your progress.

Many classes will continue to go back to the same (their favourite) venues year after year. So the quicker you get to know these the better.

A Waterproof Notebook allows you to put pen to paper immediately, and ensures that your notes remain legible whilst on the water

Checklists

Checklists can save you time and money! They allow you to do things in the most efficient way and ensure that, even in a hurry, there is little chance of an important task being forgotten. Examples would be a checklist for packing, unpacking (arriving and leaving a venue) and for both before and after racing. When the pressure is on, you are most likely to make a mistake and it never hurts to double check things.

Example Checklist
- ☐ Hull: watertight, scratch-free and down to weight.
- ☐ Covers: hull / spars / sails / masts / foils: in good condition.
- ☐ Trolley / trailer wheels and moving parts: in good order with secure straps.
- ☐ Spars (light / strong winds): check straight and look for signs of corrosion.
- ☐ Sails (light / strong winds): check for wear, ensure clean and dry, and rolled / flaked in labelled bag.
- ☐ Foils (light / strong winds): check for scratches, make sure well padded.
- ☐ Ropes: halyards and sheets – check for wear.
- ☐ Blocks and cleats: working smoothly and no need to replace.
- ☐ Spares: for all parts which need regular replacing.
- ☐ Tools: check they are present and in good order.
- ☐ Clothing: comfortable for any conditions.
- ☐ Food: high quality nutrition (especially if you have to avoid some foods), plus protein, and energy bars / drinks for stronger wind regattas, plus any necessary medications.

Advice from Double Olympic Medallist (470 class) Joe Glanfield

How much you write down depends on the person and the circumstances. If you have a lot of things going on outside of sailing, you will find that you forget things quicker and need to write more down.

I think it is very important to keep a track of the settings that you used in racing, as it stops you going in circles and making the same mistakes twice. I like to keep a log of the number of hours that I have sailed in different conditions: if there is an imbalance, I can correct this by focusing my training on the conditions I have sailed in less.

I think it is really important to write your goals down – not just your overall performance goal, but also your goals for each training session. Somehow writing them down makes you commit to them more; it also means that you can look back at them after a while and see what you were trying to achieve at different times in the year.

END NOTE

Be Your Own Sailing Coach was first published in 2008 by Wiley Nautical just in time for the Beijing Olympic Games. Originally I was approached by Tim Davison from Fernhurst at a Laser inland championship I had won. After asking me for lots of tips about the Laser, he asked if I had ever considered writing a book. At the time it was something I had never really thought about, but I had already written lots of articles for *Yachts & Yachting* and other magazines, so it was something I was happy to consider. However in 2006 Tim sold the company to John Wiley & Sons and it became Wiley Nautical, and *Be Your Own Sailing Coach* was the first book to be published by them. Seven years later Tim and a group of sailing enthusiasts bought the company back, prompting the re-working of this title into a more focused version in which I have been able to draw on my vast coaching experience since the book was first published.

I first wrote *Be Your Own Sailing Coach* whilst recovering from major neck surgery; a triple spinal fusion in my neck due to several pro-lapsed discs. It was only then that I had the time to seriously put pen to paper and I wanted to pass on my knowledge about good training techniques to as many people as possible.

The difficult thing was always deciding what to leave out, and the book was deliberately written so that you could dip in and out of it; reading and re-reading the chapters you needed to, whilst only glancing at those which were of less importance to you.

Over the last twenty years I have worked with so many different sailors, from those just starting their careers to those at their very peak. The cultural differences and backgrounds have been huge but my approach to coaching has been consistent from when I ran British Junior Zone squads to working with the eventual Laser Radial Olympic Gold Medallist, Lijia Xu from China. I use the same exercises and the same techniques, as the core skills of sailing are important regardless of class, and success is very much a combination of hard work and talent... one without the other is simply not enough.

What we have now is the more refined version: *Coach Yourself to Win*, and just as I hope that I am a better coach now than I was ten years ago, I also hope that I am a better writer. As a coach I have tried to reach out to as many people as possible but as a writer I have the opportunity to reach those I would never have the opportunity to coach.

When I was growing up the Fernhurst *Sail to Win* series was part of every serious sailor's library and it is a huge pleasure to be a part of the re-launch of this series with the new Fernhurst Books, which will include so many talented authors.

If you have enjoyed my book I hope you will find time to read *Be Your Own Tactics Coach*, as racing tactics can easily fill a book all on their own.

Wishing you successful racing. Enjoy your sailing.

Jon Emmett
2015

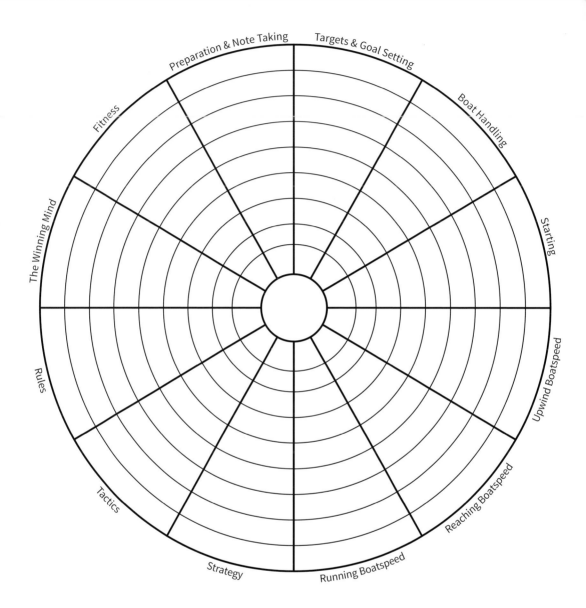

You can rate yourself on this dartboard, covering every chapter in the book

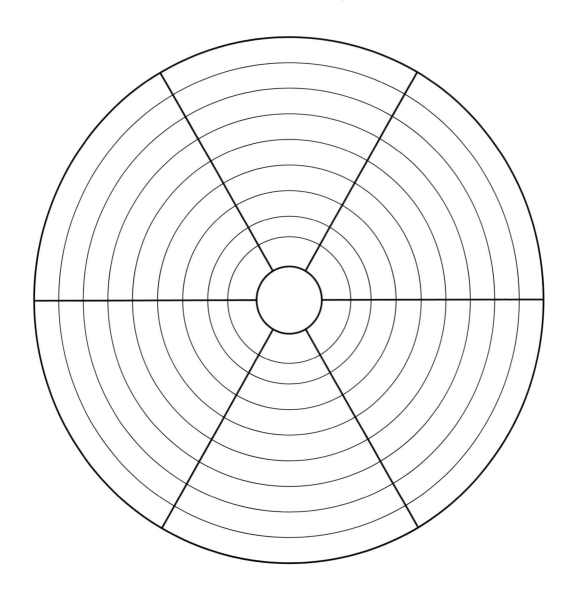

Blank dartboard for you to copy and use. Good luck!

SAIL TO WIN

Fernhurst Books are Proudly Re-launching the Iconic *Sail to Win* Series

Other titles in this series include:

Helming to Win
Nick Craig

Wind Strategy
David Houghton &
Fiona Campbell

More titles currently in development.

To find out more about the *Sail to Win* series please visit:

www.fernhurstbooks.com

Here you can also register your interest in racing and
keep up-to-date with the very latest racing news, special
offers and details of new titles.

*Simply click 'Register' on our homepage and select your
areas of interest.*